Sara Nowlan

D1528873

nur‡ure

give and get what you need to flourish

lisa bevere

workbook

Nurture Workbook

Published by: Messenger International, P.O. Box 888, Palmer Lake, CO 80133-0888.

WRITTEN AND EDITED BY:

Vincent M. Newfield
New Fields & Company
P. O. Box 622 • Hillsboro, MO 63050
www.preparethewaytoday.org

COVER, INTERIOR DESIGN & PRINT PRODUCTION:

Eastco Multi Media Solutions, Inc.
3646 California Rd.
Orchard Park, NY 14127
www.eastcomultimedia.com

Design Manager: Aaron La Porta
Designer: Heather Wierowski

Printed in Canada

Jan 30 - all music night
Feb 20 - church mt

Table of Contents

Quick Overview Instructions

*W*elcome to the *Nurture Workbook*! We're excited to bring you this fun, interactive study companion. Much prayer and many hours of work have been poured into this project. We believe the truths in this study will come alive and transform your life, as well as the lives in your sphere of influence.

This workbook contains seven chapters that correspond with the seven DVD sessions and the twelve chapters in Lisa's book. Review the instructions at the beginning of each workbook chapter to determine the corresponding DVD session to watch and book chapters to read.

FEATURES TO LOOK FOR IN EACH CHAPTER:

- **Locating Yourself** – practical, soul-searching self-tests

- **Scriptures** – powerful passages from God's Word to flesh out important truths

- **Planting Principles** – highlighted words of wisdom worth remembering

- **Activities** – creative assignments to connect you with others and apply nurture principles

- **Write Your Life** – your reflections on what God speaks to you

Throughout the workbook, you will also discover inspirational quotes from Christian leaders, poems, short stories, definitions and powerful prayers. There is also a section to journal personal notes where you can jot down your thoughts, feelings and anything else the Holy Spirit reveals to you along the *Nurture* journey. What God speaks to you through each session is *priceless* and well worth investing the time to write down.

We suggest you...

- *Begin and end each of your study sessions with prayer.* Invite the Holy Spirit to teach you and lead you into all truth (see John 16:13). When you ask, He will give you insights and understanding about what you are studying. As you finish each session, ask Him to permanently seal the truths He has revealed in your spirit and soul.

- *Read the corresponding chapters* in the *Nurture* book, watch the DVD session, and then complete the chapter in the workbook – in that order.

- *Be consistent in your study.* Whatever time and place you choose to do the workbook, stick to it. If you fall behind, don't quit. Push through to the finish. God will bless your efforts.

- *Be honest with yourself and God as you answer each question.* Knowing the truth of God's Word, along with the truth about yourself, will bring freedom to your life that can be found no other way.

The material contained in this workbook is eye-opening, challenging and life-changing. Our prayer is that you receive the nurture you need and experience a greater connection with your heavenly Father. As the gift of nurture is awakened in you, may you help awaken it in others—bringing unity and strength to the body of Christ, connecting the daughters of earth and enabling them to truly flourish in their calling!

"Nurture, the language of the feminine heart, is being restored as women arise, recognize each other and begin to connect for strength and purpose."
~Lisa Bevere

Why Nurture

Read chapters 1 and 2 in the *Nurture* book and view DVD session 1.

Understanding Nurture and the Power it Possesses

nurture
1. To give *tender care* and *protection* to a child, a young animal or a plant, helping it grow and develop.
2. To *encourage* somebody or something to grow, develop, thrive and be successful.[1]

Locating Yourself

"AM I IN NEED OF NURTURE?"
Circle a number from 1 to 5—1 being "I strongly agree"; 5 being "I strongly disagree."

1. I believe my mom loved me with all her heart, but she always seemed so busy, so we never really connected.
   (1) 2 3 4 5

2. Even now I feel the need for a mother figure.
   1 (2) 3 4 5

3. I don't have anyone speaking encouragement, correction or direction into my life on a regular basis.
   1 2 (3) 4 5

Planting PRINCIPLE

"The need for *connection* is often more viable than the need for food. And as women, we have the ability to connect people. I think, as the Church, we have lost the ability to understand the importance of connection. People need to know that they are *watched for*. People need to know that they are *welcomed*. People need to know they are *safe* and that somebody is going to make sure they *have what they need* to make it."

[session 1]

4. If my children, grandchildren or someone younger than me is hurt or in trouble, I tend to clam up because I really don't know what to say.

1 2 ③ 4 5

5. Feelings of fear, doubt and insecurity seem to hang over me like a cloud. I can't seem to escape from its dark shadow.

1 2 ③ 4 5

> **GRADE:** Add the numbers you circled in each question. If your score is…
>
> **5-10:** You will greatly benefit as you begin to open your heart to be nurtured.
>
> **11-19:** You are receiving some nurturing, and as you seek more, your life will begin to blossom even further.
>
> **20-25:** You are growing and reaching full bloom and becoming well-equipped to nurture others.

1. Just as the baby bird in P.D. Eastman's story was filled with questions, you too may be in search for answers to life. In your inner quest to be connected, what questions are swirling around in you?

    can e be unselfish long enough to show my children the nurture and love they need? How can e be less busy in order to nurture?

2. There are *three* main ingredients to nurture—*tender care, protection* and *encouragement.* What do these words mean to you?

    Tender Care is … _holding your sick child. putting all else aside to meet the urgent needs of someone who is hurting. Putting love into action._

    Protection means … _doing everything necessary to keep someone safe even if it means putting yourself in harms way._

    To **Encourage** is to … _Speak words of life to someone. To cheer on; cheer up. Letting them know they can do it and everythings gonna be alright_

Your PART

"Nurture is not expensive—it is *expansive*. The life of everyone enlarges when nurture is added… Nurture has the power to enlarge or awaken areas of your life that will make significant contributions. Any gift, ability, or talent we have is given to us to improve and enhance the lives of others. There is something within you that this world desperately needs." [pages 14, 19]

It's time to discover your gifts, abilities and talents. Pause here to make a list of the areas in your life that are waiting to be nurtured and lended strength. Look for opportunities at home, church and in your community where you can use them to nurture the gifts in others.

musical abilities to be able to help ← *this is "Nurture in the Spirit!"* ☺

Others enter worship in spirit & truth
self worth/ knowing inner beauty —
helping others see themselves
as God sees them
being more others centered & Christ centered
rather than self centered — friend to
encouragement   the friend-less

3. Children are very impressionable. Can you remember an encounter from your childhood when your mother, grandmother or someone else said or did something to nurture the gifts and talents in you? Who was it, what did they do, and how are their actions still impacting others through you today?

_____

_____

_____

_____

4. Teachers play a powerful role in the lives of children. Can you think of a past teacher who showed you the true meaning of nurture? Describe their actions and how their life influenced and affected yours. How is your life still being shaped by their influence today?

Mr. DeVries saw that I was headed down
the wide path - off the narrow - he sat me
down & encouraged me to be who I am in
Christ - a new creation - don't take on the
old yucky world. I didn't listen then - I
gave into rebellion but it still means alot to me

that he took time to obey God & speak wisdom into my life

5. If you find yourself guarded toward others and focused on just trying to survive day-to-day life, it may be that you were wounded by someone you reached out to for nurturing. Ask the Lord to show you why you're hesitant and withdrawn from others. Write what He reveals and surrender it to Him in prayer.

Felt like I was alone during deployment certainly wasn't nurtured by Danny then. Not sure if I'm guarded - and I do feel like I'm trying to just survive day-to-day life - I am aware I am extremely self-involved.

6. Pruning can be painful, but it is an indispensable part of the nurturing process. Explain the importance of pruning as it relates to nurture and identify the difference between being *cut back* and *cut off*.

If God didn't prune us He'd not be nurturing us - He shows us tender care by pruning protects us so we don't become unfruitful & get cut off - encourages us by reminding us pruning is only a cut back - not a cut off and He's only doing it because He wants us to be fruitful.

He cuts off every branch of mine that doesn't produce fruit, and he prunes the branches that do bear fruit so they will produce even more. Remain in me, and I will remain in you. For a branch cannot produce fruit if it is severed from the vine, and you cannot be fruitful unless you <u>remain in me.</u>

~John 15:2,4 NLT vs.2

7. One word that could be used to describe the meaning of nurture is *relationship*. Describe some of the differences between just meeting someone's needs and actually nurturing them. What is your nurturing role in the season you are currently in?

Caring more about their needs than yours I am of course deep into needing to nurture my children - also really need to nurture Danny however I can. Not just saying I care or I'll pray for those in need but really praying and putting action to the care.

8. Clearly, women hold the key to nurturing the sons and daughters of the earth. With this in mind, how do you think the women's liberation movement of the past few decades has affected the need for nurturing? How has it affected you personally?

womens lib says we dont need nurture probably has instilled in me a desire to be self-sufficient, self-indulgent, all about me It says you can be super mom & worker & wife & friend but without nurture you cant!

9. Romans 12:16 in the Amplified Bible says that we are to live in harmony with one another—readily *adjusting* ourselves to people and things. What are some of the adjustments or changes that you see need to take place in your family in order for your grandmother, mother and the daughters to all unite and have "one voice" and lend each other strength?

? building up not tearing down encouraging not judging being selfless relinquish control to the Holy Spirit!

Planting
PRINCIPLE

"Mothers help us discover who we are. You can't allow just anyone to define you. You should not ask just anything who you are or whom you belong to. You should ask questions only of those you know have answers. ...In an atmosphere of nurture, the answers are revealed. There are *answers* with true mothers. There is *safety* when true mothers enfold us, even if they are not sure they can answer all the questions. We need the comfort and assurance of their presence. The truth is, there has never been a more desperate need for the presence of nurture."

[pages 8, 9]

Greater love has no one than this,
that he lay down his life for his friends.
~John 15:13 NIV

10. As a mature woman of God, it's important to be on the lookout for other women who are in need of nurture. Name three people in your circle of influence who are searching for nurture from you. If possible, write down the kind of nurture they're looking for.

Heather - Heather & Christy -
Heather - friendship/tender care
Amy - all areas/need to be a good example
my kids - all areas
Sharon - encouragement
Sarah & other youth girls - all areas

11. Women today often wear many hats and have a keen ability to multitask well. However, it is important to keep our priorities in order. Take a moment and (honestly) list your top 10 priorities as they currently exist. Then in the second column, prayerfully rearrange your priorities in the order you feel God can best bless.

TOP 10 PRIORITIES As you currently live	TOP 10 PRIORITIES—REMIX Your priorities the way you want to live
1. Kids	1. God
2. house/responsibilities	2. Danny
3. friends/family	3. Kids
4. Clients	4. church
5. Danny	5. friends/family
6. God - our relationship	6. house/responsibilities
7. Church	7. clients
8.	8.
9.	9.
10.	10.

12. When it comes to nurturing, what unique God-given ability do you have as a woman?

Spirit of discernment - usually can sense when someone needs encouragement.

13. In your own words, describe what it means to flourish. In light of your definition, would you say that you are flourishing? If not, ask the Lord to show you why.

Do not strive/struggle. To run the race without hesitation or distraction. I'm not flourishing because my priorities are out of whack — also I have been trying to escape reality because reality hurts right now.

to fulfill God's destiny for your life

He will complete the work in me if I let Him!

14. There are a number of "big things" happening among women today. Name a few of the positive doors of opportunity you see opening that have been closed for years.

Activity

At The Movies

It is very important to understand and get a good grasp on the *nature* of nurture. Slowly reread the definition of nurture. Now stop and think: If you could pick a movie that powerfully impacted you with a true picture of nurture, what would it be? What scene or quote from that movie is etched in your mind as illustrating nurture? Describe it and explain why you chose it. [If you are in a group study, we suggest securing one or two of the movies selected; cue up the individual scene(s), view them together and discuss them as a group.] Example: In the movie *August Rush*, the young orphan boy was asked the question: "What do you want to be in the world?" After pondering this a moment, he simply answered, "Found."

NAME OF MOVIE _____

Description of scene selected

_____

_____

_____

_____

_____

_____

I chose this scene because...

_____

_____

_____

_____

_____

Making Connections

So encourage each other and build each other up,
just as you are already doing.
~1 Thessalonians 5:11 NLT vs.2

How do you feel when someone gives you a comment of encouragement when you're down or disappointed? Indeed, it is like a cool breeze on a hot summer's day—*energizing* and *refreshing*—that penetrates deep within. Look around you. Someone somewhere needs your encouragement right now—maybe even your daughter or son who is all grown up and moved away. Ask the Lord to show you who He can encourage through you, and ask Him to give you the words to write a letter that will touch their heart. You may also want to include a Scripture or two. Once you write the letter, hold it in your hands and pray a blessing of God's encouragement to be given to the recipient.

...he who refreshes others will himself be refreshed.
~Proverbs 11:25 NIV

In order to nurture, I have to accept nurture.

Daughter of the King, you are loved by your heavenly Father more than words can say! He can clearly see all the awesome gifts and powerful potential within you—He is the one who put them there. If no one has ever told you how valuable and special you are, take a moment and ask the Father, "What do You see in me?" Let Him write a description on your heart that will enlarge every area of your life. Write down His expressions of love to you in the space below.

gift of mercy
not shy
can show others love / encouragement
desire to have a pure heart
a past full of God's deliverance
a future full of His power
can help others find the beauty in themselves

How precious it is, Lord, to realize that you are thinking about me constantly!
I can't even count how many times a day your thoughts turn toward me.
And when I waken in the morning, you are still thinking of me!
~Psalm 139:17-18 TLB

---

1. *Merriam Webster's Desk Dictionary* (Springfield, MA: Merriam Webster, Incorporated 1995).

notes from session 1

I have never felt more free and empowered as a woman. I know that NOW
IS THE TIME to write my life and connect with others around me.
~todaystrendsetter, TX

Making Your Connections

2

Read chapters 3 and 4 in the *Nurture* book and view DVD session 2.

The Need for Relationships and How to Establish Them

> *Connecting*
> "I believe there is such a desperate need for healthy connections among women of all ages. Everywhere I travel, the breakdown seems increasingly evident. Far too many women are disconnected and isolated. Others want desperately to connect but just don't know how to see this happen. It may be awkward at first, but it must start somewhere. The mothers need to watch for daughters and the daughters need to watch for mothers, and when they recognize each other they need to take the time to make that God-breathed connection—at whatever level or opportunity it presents itself." [page 51]

1. With thoughtfulness and detail, Lisa offered expanded definitions of a *daughter, mother* and *grandmother*. What characteristics in each of these descriptions mean the most to you personally? Why?

Daughter _mother's treasure – because that's what I want to be to my mama & what I want Nora to be to me._

Mother _lay down life to bring forth life – because I desire to do this – but I need gods help to not be selfish!_

Grandmother *Gnardians of perspective, secrets & insight — because I want them to share & teach me these things.*

2. With each successive role women hold, there is a specific purpose and function. Explain briefly the function of each and give the "word" that seems to be ever-present in their mouth. In which position or positions do you find yourself?

Daughter *"Why?" growing, need to ask for things such as) connection, love, affirmation & answers*

Mother *"Because" – grown; have answers, meet needs, give love, ask for obedience, and are often busy*

Grandmother *"Let it go, it doesn't matter" they almost embody maternal love & life answers*

I believe my position is *daughter & mother*

Planting PRINCIPLE

"All of us are daughters. We may become a wife, a mother, a grandmother, and if we are really blessed, a great-grand-mother. But you are always a daughter; you never lose the standing of a daughter with God. I believe we need to re-store dignity back to all of these positions."

[adapted from session 2]

3. What are some of the things you appreciate most about your mom? If you were being interviewed on prime time TV and were asked to thank her for the *number one* thing she taught you, what would you say?

to love God & seek Him

4. Maybe your biological mother was unable to offer you all the loving, caring nurture you needed and God intended you to have. If so, He probably sent someone else into your life to fill in the gaps. Who became a *mother* to you? What specific things did she do that helped you connect with her?

    _____

    _____

    _____

    _____

> Anyone who does the will of my Father in heaven
> is my brother and sister and mother!
> **~Matthew 12:50 NLT**

Connecting

"There is something about people who are related in the spirit. When we see each other, we recognize each other because we know each other by the spirit. Anyone who does God's will is related to Jesus... But the promise does not stop there; we are not only related to Jesus, we are related to others who are doing the will of God along the same lines. When God *relates* people, it is for increased personal strength, spiritual growth, and kingdom purposes."

[adapted from session 2 and page 43]

5. Look over the landscape of your life. What women has the Lord brought into your life with longing in their eyes for acceptance, love, encouragement and direction? These are *daughters* who are looking for a mother. Who do *you* desire to be a daughter of? — *my clients* → *anyone who loves God & will love me as I am & teach me!*

    empathy - listening/praying for people
    ↳ this is nurture even if I don't say anything, its nurture in the spirit!

6. What words of encouragement and actions of affection are the *daughters* looking, longing and craving to receive from *mothers*? Be on the lookout to invest these priceless possessions into the precious lives of those who need it so desperately.

    to be heard, understood, accepted, loved
    beautiful
    giving of yourself shows that what you say is true

7. Have you ever withheld nurture from a sister in Christ? If yes, why? In prayer, ask the Holy Spirit to search your heart and reveal the root reasons.

_____

_____

_____

_____

Locating Yourself

WHAT'S KEEPING ME FROM CONNECTING?
Read each statement and circle True or False.

1. It hurts me to see a friend achieve success or be richly blessed; at times it even makes me angry. The more someone else is blessed, the more I hate to be around them.
   TRUE or FALSE

2. There are few things I enjoy more than getting the inside scoop on what's happening in the lives of others. I usually don't repeat things, but I love to listen!
   TRUE or FALSE

3. It's so hard to get my mind off my problems. I'm so overwhelmed by the things I'm dealing with that I just don't have the time to help anybody else. Besides, I feel safer being alone.
   TRUE or FALSE

4. I feel as though I am in a constant contest with certain people I know. I'm always trying to wear the latest fashions, drive the newest car, and be in the know about current events.
   TRUE or FALSE

5. I believe that when I find and marry the man who's meant for me, everything else in my life will fall into place. Therefore, I will do whatever it takes to get him.
   TRUE or FALSE

GRADE: If you answered TRUE to any of the questions, it may be that your ability to connect with others is being blocked by one or more of these: envy, gossip, isolation, competition or men.

8. Trying to force a relationship to flourish can be a struggle and strain, but allowing God to establish divine connections is *life giving*. After hearing and reading about godly connections, can you see some of the divine connections God has established, or is trying to establish, in your life? Who are they with?

Heather McCullough   Allison Hurley
Beverlay Hess

Pruning

"You need to know who your friends are. The Bible says that bad company corrupts good morals (1 Corinthians 15:33). So we need to be women who find out who the 'good company' is—who are the women we can build with? You cannot build with, be affiliated with, or have alliances with the people who are going to have bad morals."

[adapted from session 2]

Who are you in relationship with who you know in your heart is bad company? Who do you hang out with who tends to drag you down spiritually? It's time to get out the social pruning shears and sever any relationship that you know in your heart is holding you back in your walk with the Lord.

No one who is born of God will continue to sin, because *God's seed remains in him;* he cannot go on sinning, because he has been born of God.

~1 John 3:9 NIV
[Italics added for emphasis.]

9. There is a *seed* of heaven in the life of every woman, and as a grandmother, mother, sister or daughter in God's family you must seek to purposely bless and nurture these seeds. In what practical ways can you bless and nurture the divine seed of God in others *within the house of God*? What about *outside your church*, such as at school, work and in the community? (pages 42, 43)

I can bless women INSIDE the church by...

seeing them & loving them as they are
and not judging — not gossiping

I can bless women OUTSIDE the church by...

shining my light - being true to my faith - loving, caring, serving unconditionally

Whenever we have the opportunity, we should do good to everyone, especially to our Christian brothers and sisters.

~**Galatians 6:10 NLT**

Planting
PRINCIPLE

"It will take many mothers (and fathers) to successfully raise the daughters of this generation, just as it takes many fathers (and mothers) to raise the sons who now walk the earth. Their season of nurture may be short, but it must be potent and concentrated if this generation of promise is to accomplish the God-breathed destinies woven into the fabric of their beings."

[page 41]

10. Men *and* women are needed to fulfill God's eternal plans and purposes. It is the sons and daughters *together* who reflect the fullness of God's image in human form (Genesis 1:27). Briefly explain the role each play in God's plan and why they need to work together to see it come to pass. (page 63)

men - strength
women - heart

'In the last days, God said, I will pour out my Spirit upon all people. Your sons *and daughters* will prophesy, your young men will see visions, and your old men will dream dreams. In those days I will pour out my Spirit upon all my servants, men *and women* alike, and they will prophesy. And I will cause wonders in the heavens above and signs on the earth below...'

~**Acts 2:17-19 NLT**
[Italics added for emphasis.]

11. From Eve, Rahab and Ruth in the Old Testament, to Elizabeth, Anna and Mary in the New Testament, God has *always* included women in His plan to redeem mankind. In what ways were women uniquely and intimately a part of Jesus' death, burial and resurrection that men were *not* a part of? (pages 60, 61)

at His feet at the cross, preparing His body - at the tomb weeping, when angels announced He's alive!

12. To experience a real sharpening among fellow sisters in Christ, what conditions must be met? What things are really not that important?

be like-minded (iron sharpens iron, not iron sharpens steel) the outer package of the person.

> As iron sharpens iron, a friend sharpens a friend.
> **~Proverbs 27:17 NLT**

13. Name the six major hindrances that can keep you from connecting with other sisters in Christ. Which one(s) do you struggle with most? Why?

self-absorption   gossip   men
envy   isolation
jealousy   distrust fear/intimidation

Your PART

"We need to find out what God has called us to do. And then we need to get with the women who have similar [spiritual] DNA, and we need to begin to hone each other. …We need to be people who align ourselves with strength after we've aligned ourselves with heaven. I believe God has heavenly allegiances and alliances for each of you."

[session 2]

Do you want God's best for your life and the lives of others? Then keep your eyes open for His divine connections—other women of faith with similar strengths, goals and passions whom you seem to easily "click" with. God is gathering and preparing daughters, mothers and grandmothers for the end-time harvest and His soon return. Who is He trying to connect you with, and what role are you to play in each of their lives?

Activity

Sister to Sister!

> For where two or three gather together because
> they are mine, I am there among them.
> **~Matthew 18:20 NLT**

Who do you know who shares your core beliefs, goals and passions? Who are you drawn to so strongly that it seems you are related? These are sisters you can *play* with and *pray* with—you can laugh with and learn with. Prayerfully and carefully form a group with a few of these sisters in Christ who are like-minded. You may start with two or three, but be open to adding others as the Lord leads. Plan a regular get-together in a non-threatening environment where each of you can openly and honestly share your joys, sorrows, highs and lows of life. *Listen* to others as they share their hearts. Your outlook will be honed and your comfort zones challenged—your life will not be the same.

Connecting

"Other women are watching for you! They want to be your friends. They are just not sure how to approach you. Perhaps they are at your school. Maybe there are women searching for friends in the marketplace. I know the daughters in the house of God are looking for companions. Women the world over are looking for someone who will understand their hopes and fears as only another woman can. Open your eyes and look around you. I believe God is in the process of connecting His daughters with each other, with mothers, and with grandmothers. He is establishing relationships and family dynamics among His people. This is where we will find our places of strength. As we link together, weaknesses will be minimized and assets maximized." [pages 66, 67]

> The heartfelt counsel of a friend is as sweet as perfume and incense.
> **~Proverbs 27:9 NLT**

Making Connections

*Let him who receives instruction in the Word [of God] share all
good things with his teacher [contributing to his support].*
~Galatians 6:6 AMP

What women of God have inspired you? Whose passion and challenging words have awakened new possibilities in you and created a fresh hunger in your heart to believe God for greater things? Take time to **write a letter of appreciation** to one of these "Mothering Maidens." When you send it, you may even want to include a gift or some other form of an *offering of thanks* to tangibly express your gratefulness to her for richly sowing into your life. The impact of your letter in the hands of the Holy Spirit will be powerful!

My mama, JoAnn Taylor

Positioning Yourself

"Women are so amazing in the plan of God. He has always included us in His redemptive plan. But it was not enough for us to just be a part of His redemptive plan. It is our season to be a part of His return. God is building you, as a living stone, into His spiritual temple—our heavenly Father is honing our individual stones so that we can be built into a collective habitation for His Spirit to abide. Now is the time to be connected."

[adapted from session 2]

Precious princess of the kingdom of heaven, your life matters to the Most High, and He has a definite place in His plan for you. What is the Lord doing in your life right now to prepare you for His return? What relationships is He asking you to prune from your life? Who is He asking you to connect with—to be a daughter or a mother to? Are you willing to be flexible in His hands?

Write YOUR LIFE

"You rarely find women uniting or expressing friendship with peers in a deep, meaningful way. They more frequently appear as jealous rivals jockeying for position and affection! Upon discovering this, I had to ask: 'Why? Were women never meant to be friends?' Frustrated, I cried out to God and this is how He answered: 'The chapter of the daughters is being written right now. Tell My daughters to *write their lives well.*'"

[adapted from page 57]

God has a wonderful plan for your life! It starts and is sustained through intimacy with Him and overflows into intimacy with others who also bear His image and share His purposes. Has God given you a dream? Has He spoken something specific to you about His plan for your life? If He has, write it out. If He hasn't, get quiet before Him and ask Him to reveal it.

He is calling me to clean up so He can use me. He's calling me to prepare musically so I can share the songs He's giving me.

"For I know the plans I have for you," says the Lord. "They are plans for good
and not for disaster, to give you a future and a hope."
~**Jeremiah 29:11 NLT**

notes from session 2

The busyness of life, sin, pain and greed have distorted our views of each other. Many of us are unaware of how to nurture others and we are unfamiliar with what it is to be nurtured. Yet, I so believe we can change that tide and I realize that it starts with my own life.

~K.F., MO

Recovering Intuition 3

Read chapters 5 and 6 in the *Nurture* book and view DVD session 3.

Learning How to Use Your God-given Sense of Discernment

Locating Yourself

WHAT'S MY *HEART* CONDITION?

Circle a number from 1 to 5 [1 = Almost always; 2 = Often; 3 = Sometimes; 4 = Seldom; 5 = Never].

1. I serve the Lord with my whole heart. I don't hold anything back from Him or put anything before Him. [See Deuteronomy 6:5; Mark 12:29-30.]
   1 2 3 4 5

2. I hear and heed the voice of God's Spirit—I am sensitive to His touch and obedient to His request. [See Ezekiel 11:19-20.]
   1 2 3 4 5

3. I seek the heart of God in the decisions I make; He is the first person I turn to for direction. [See Proverbs 3:5-7; Matthew 6:33.]
   1 2 3 4 5

4. When I do wrong, I am convicted; I quickly turn to God to repent, ask for His forgiveness, and am restored into right relationship with Him. [See 1 John 1:9-10.]
   1 2 3 4 5

5. I am confident and at peace in my relationship with the Father; I fearlessly and boldly approach His throne in prayer anytime, anywhere, about anything. [See Hebrews 4:15-16; Ephesians 3:12; 6:18.]
   1 2 3 4 5

> **GRADE:** Add the numbers you circled in each question. If your score is…
>
> **5-10:** Your heart condition is healthy and will continue to grow freer and stronger as you stay close to the Father's heart.
>
> **11-19:** Your heart is functioning, but it's not yet at peak performance. Open yourself up to the healing of the Holy Spirit.
>
> **20-25:** Your heart is hurting and in need of nurture from your Father in heaven and His daughters here on earth.

Behold, You desire truth in the inner being; make me
therefore to know wisdom in my inmost heart.
~**Psalm 51:6 AMP**

1. Truth is the indispensable foundation of everything in life. Without it, everything is unstable and unsure. In your own words, write what it means to *be true*. In what specific areas do you find it difficult to be truthful with *yourself*? How about with *others*?

   _____

   _____

   _____

   _____

2. What naturally results in your relationship with others when you are *true* to yourself? And what naturally results when you are *untrue* to yourself?

   _____

   _____

   _____

   _____

Pruning

"If we want clarity and truth, then our murky waters must first be purified if they are to be found clean and true. If a source or core is tainted, all that issues forth from it is likewise polluted. When it comes to the human dynamic, the heart is the place where truth is secured and falsehood confronted. ...Daughters, it stands to reason that if the source or well we draw from is salty or untrue, then the water we pour forth is likewise unwholesome. Out of the abundance of our hearts our mouths will speak." (see Luke 6:45.)

[page 81]

What's the condition of your heart? Are you filled with bitterness, resentment and unforgiveness over the pain of the past? Is your heart hard and immovable in the hands of the Lord, or is it soft and sensitive to His touch? Maybe it's time to call upon Him to help you clean house. He will show you what to keep and what to get rid of and give you the strength to do it. All you have to do is ask.

Keep and guard your heart with all vigilance and above all
that you guard, for out of it flow the springs of life.
~Proverbs 4:23 AMP

3. When you repent of your sins and invite Jesus into your heart, your spirit is reborn—you become a *new creation*, God gives you a *new heart*, and His Spirit makes His home in you (see John 3:3-6, 14:23; 2 Corinthians 5:17; Ezekiel 11:19-20). But while your spirit, or heart, is made totally new, your soul—which is your mind, will and emotions—still needs work. What specific things can you do to renew your soul?

    _____
    _____
    _____
    _____
    _____
    _____
    _____
    _____
    _____
    _____

4. As you hide the Word of God in your heart through reading, studying and meditating, it will *transform* you from the inside out. Look up the Scriptures below and write the specific benefit or effect of having God's Word inscribed on the tablet of your heart.

    Joshua 1:8 _____

    Psalm 119:11 _____

    Psalm 119:105 _____

    Jeremiah 23:29 _____

    John 8:31-32 _____

    John 17:17 _____

    Hebrews 4:12 _____

    James 1:21 _____

Your PART

"If the heart is transcribed with truth, it will ordain (proclaim and order) or prophesy (reveal God's will) in life. If your heart is on target, then your future is secure. This is crucial because most Christians know where they are going but they have no idea how to get there! The Word of God becomes the director of our paths."

[page 87]

Hiding God's Word in your heart is not an option—it is a necessity. Ask the Holy Spirit to show you some practical ways to get the Word in your heart while at home, in your car, and at work.

Let not *mercy* and *truth* forsake you; bind them around your neck,
write them on the *tablet of your heart*, and so find favor
and high esteem in the sight of God and man.
~**Proverbs 3:3-4 NKJV**
[Boldness and italics added for emphasis.]

intuition

1. The state of being aware of or knowing something without having to discover or perceive it, or the ability to do this.
2. Something known or believed instinctively, without actual evidence for it.
3. Immediate knowledge of something.[1]

5. Many times God's Spirit living inside of you will direct you through your intuition. Describe the difference between *intuition* and *suspicion*. What feelings are usually connected with each? Look up and memorize Philippians 4:8—a perfect prescription for helping you focus on what's good while staying free from suspicion.

_____

_____

_____

_____

_____

_____

_____

_____

Connecting

"The Latin breakdown of *intuition* (*in* and *tueor*) yields "inward tutor," which is perfectly confirmed by Scripture (see 1 John 2:27). When truth is spoken the inward tutor, or the Holy Spirit of God, confirms it to you and in you. There is a distinct prompting and a release of life. You will feel a resounding "Yes, listen and receive this" inside of you. You will feel as though light and strength, truth and freedom are being poured out upon you. ...This can happen as you read, worship, pray, hear a sermon, drive your car, take a shower, or speak with a close friend."

[pages 103, 104]

6. Look back over your life. Have you ever had a "feeling" that something wasn't right about a certain person or situation but you pushed the warning away? Explain what happened and what kept you from following your intuition.

_____

_____

_____

_____

_____

7. It's very important to know whether the inner signals you're receiving are God's *intuition* or the enemy's *suspicion*. Read James 3:17 and list the eight characteristics of *godly wisdom* that confirm when you're hearing from God.

_____

_____

_____

_____

_____

_____

If you need wisdom—if you want to know what God wants you
to do—ask him, and he will gladly tell you. He will not resent your asking.
But when you ask him, be sure that you really expect him to answer,
for a doubtful mind is as unsettled as a wave of the sea
that is driven and tossed by the wind.
~James 1:5-6 NLT

8.   Decisions, decisions—you make them all the time about all kinds of things. What do you normally do when you're faced with making a decision and need to know the right thing to do? **Read** James 1:5-7 and Proverbs 3:4-8 and write out the basic instructions God gives for receiving wisdom and direction for your life.

_____

_____

_____

_____

_____

_____

9.   If there is ever a time you need wisdom and direction, it is when you're faced with overwhelming difficulties and conflicts. To confront them accurately and effectively, you must have the intuition of God's Spirit leading you in what to do. Do you have a persistent problem with a person in your life that you can't seem to conquer? Explain the situation. Prayerfully commit it to God and ask Him for wisdom on what to do.

_____

Planting PRINCIPLE

"Daughters, you will come up against many problems and conflicts. You may be tempted to take many of them personally. I implore you, fight this temptation. These issues and asides will never be successfully navigated from a personal perspective. Stop exhausting yourself trying to make sense of the senseless situations you've been through. Don't take it personal—it's not about you. It's all about what's going on inside of the other person."
[adapted from session 3 and chapter 6]

For we are not fighting against people made of flesh and blood, but against the evil rulers and authorities of the unseen world, against those mighty powers of darkness who rule this world, and against wicked spirits in the heavenly realms.
~Ephesians 6:12 NLT

10. Recall a situation in which you either *didn't* seek God for direction or you chose not to follow the direction He gave you. Explain what happened and what you learned from it.

_____

_____

_____

Now recall a situation in which you earnestly sought the Lord for direction over an important decision, and His counsel saved you from experiencing major heartache.

_____

_____

_____

Connecting

"God is the source of all intuition, discernment, and understanding. He gives it and He can take it away. This is not about an exercise of human self-actualization, but a *connection* with the divine and holy One. A fraction of the enlightenment of heaven is shed abroad in our earthen vessels by the power of the Holy Spirit when we become daughters of heaven."

[page 106]

---

11. Jesus says in Matthew 5:14, "**You** are the *light* of the world." Take a moment and think about all the different lights in your life. Consider the lights in each room of your home, on your appliances, and on your car, as well as things like street lights, sunlight and a lighthouse. List at least *five* benefits you receive from light and explain how they symbolically relate to you being the *light of the world*.

Light benefits me by...	Spiritually, this *benefit* symbolically demonstrates...
_____	_____
_____	_____
_____	_____
_____	_____
_____	_____

*Let your light so shine before men, that they may see your
good works and glorify your Father in heaven.*
~Matthew 5:16 NKJV

Planting
PRINCIPLE

"We do not just minister the
Word—we minister what is in
us. Therefore, we want to make
sure that what we release is refreshing and attractive and light
to everybody. People need to
know us as light—not as rule-
givers, not as darkness, not as
judgmental, not as critical, but
as light. Light is attractive—it
draws other people. Light
makes people want to gather."
[adapted from session 3]

12. In what practical ways do you *shine* as a light to others and draw people to Jesus? In what places and situations and to what people do you find it *easier* to shine? Why do you think this is the case?

_____

_____

_____

_____

_____

_____

_____

13. On the other hand, in what ways have you *hidden* God's light in you from shining? In what places and to what people do you find it *harder* to shine? Get quiet before the Lord and ask Him to show you the reasons why. Write what He reveals.

_____

_____

_____

_____

_____

_____

_____

*A good man produces good deeds from a good heart.
And an evil man produces evil deeds from his hidden wickedness.
Whatever is in the heart overflows into speech.*
~Luke 6:45 TLB
[Italics added for emphasis.]

14. As a daughter of God, you are "to give light to those who sit in darkness and in the shadow of death, and to guide [them] to the path of peace" (Luke 1:79 NLT). What conditions are needed in your life in order to *give light* to others and create an atmosphere for intuition to flourish?

_____

_____

_____

_____

_____

15. The gift of intuition is precious and priceless. If you have lost this God-given ability, what steps can you take to recover it?

_____

_____

_____

_____

_____

_____

Positioning Yourself

"Women are God's answer to hurting relationships, a dying world, and an impotent church. Women are God's beautiful problem solvers. …You, daughter, are an agent of truth who cannot afford to distrust the light within you. Doubt is one of the mightiest weapons your enemy raises against you. It will cause you to hesitate and waiver in unbelief and fear. Press in and get the counsel of heaven."

[page 101]

prayer

Heavenly Father, thank You for opening my eyes to this powerful truth about the gift of intuition. Please sharpen my listening skills so that I may clearly hear Your voice speaking to me. Help me distinguish the difference between suspicion and intuition and faithfully act upon Your promptings. Give me the grace to fearlessly and lovingly shine the light of truth for all to see. In Jesus' name, Amen.

It's Time to Remove the Basket!

> You are the light of the world. A city that is set on a hill cannot
> be hidden. Nor do they light a lamp and put it under a basket,
> but on a lampstand, and it gives light to all who are in the house.
> **~Matthew 5:14-15 NKJV**

In Jesus' day, people used small clay lamps filled with olive oil with a wick in the center to light their homes. Since the amount of light they gave off was very limited, the lamps were strategically placed high on a "lampstand," which was often a small nook cut out of the wall.[2] To place a basket or a bowl over a lamp would be foolish because the light would be covered and, in many cases, snuffed out altogether.

* *Take a few moments to answer these questions individually and then discuss them as a group.*

Since you received Christ into your life, what "baskets" have others tried to put over the light of God's Spirit in you?

_____

_____

_____

_____

_____

_____

Have you put any "baskets" over yourself (these are the places of shadow)? If so, what are they?

_____

_____

_____

_____

_____

_____

What "baskets" have you knowingly or unknowingly tried to put on others?

_____

_____

_____

_____

_____

On the flipside, what have others said or done that fueled the fire of God's light in you?

_____

_____

_____

_____

REFLECT

What new perspective do you now have after hearing others in the group share their experiences?

_____

_____

_____

_____

_____

Your PART

"God is challenging us to release the light and life that have been quickened within each of us. Some of us have quenched the light of our God-given feminine intuition and it needs to be reignited."

[page 92]

Making Connections

…I want you to be wise about what is good, and innocent about what is evil.
~Romans 16:19 NIV

We can't go on together with suspicious minds—the title of a well-known song and also a powerful truth. There is no way we can function in a healthy relationship with another person if we are suspicious of them. If we are suspicious of their motives and their actions, we will eventually gather enough "dirt" on them (often perceived and not real) that we will sever the relationship.

Has this happened to you? Have you ever broken off a relationship on the grounds of suspicion with someone who was once a good friend? Remember, suspicion is "the act or an instance of suspecting something wrong without proof"[3] and is rooted in *worry* and *fear*—not the God-given intuition of the Holy Spirit.

Write a letter of apology to the person the Holy Spirit is bringing to your mind—the woman who was once a trusted friend, but is no longer your friend because you severed the relationship out of suspicion. Be honest, share your heart, point out a number of good qualities she has, and ask her to forgive you. When you do, you will strengthen the body of Christ and experience a new level of freedom and inner healing in your life.

…Fix your thoughts on what is true and good and right. Think about things that are pure and lovely, and dwell on the fine, good things in others. Think about all you can praise God for and be glad about.
~Philippians 4:8 TLB

Write YOUR LIFE

Has this week's lesson on recovering intuition been eye-opening for you? What is the Holy Spirit revealing to you about your heart's condition? How has the connection between intuition and the Spirit's role in your life as the "inward tutor" become clearer? What action is the Holy Spirit prompting you to take?

_____

_____

_____

_____

_____

1. *Merriam Webster's Desk Dictionary* (Springfield, MA: Merriam Webster, Incorporated 1995). 2. *NIV Archeological Study Bible* (Grand Rapids, MI: The Zondervan Corporation, 2005) see note at Matthew 5:15. 3. See note 1.

notes from session 3

I recommend this book to every woman who desires to leave a legacy. It's been on my heart to present a gift of timeless love and purposeful life to not only my daughters, but to everyone our Lord puts in my path. Lisa makes you want to join her in awakening women to be who they were created to be. This book has ignited something in me.

~M.B., CO

Bringing It Home

Read chapters 7 and 8 in the *Nurture* book and view DVD special session, *Bringing It Home*.

Bridging the Generational Gap and Leaving a Legacy

AM I MORE OF A *MENTOR* OR A *MOTHER*?

Choose the words or phrases that best represent you in the questions below.

1. Do I tend to merely reproduce myself in others, **or** do I desire greater things for them?

   _____

2. Am I more of a spectator of others, **or** am I personally involved in their lives?

   _____

3. Do others see me as a professional counselor **or** someone who is real and connected to them?

   _____

4. Is the time I spend with others primarily scheduled, **or** am I flexible and available even when it is inconvenient for me?

   _____

5. Do I only allow others to see my successes, **or** am I open to sharing my weaknesses and what I've learned from my failures?

   _____
   _____
   _____

> **GRADE:** If you selected the *first* option more often, you tend to be more of a *mentor* to the women God brings into your life. If you selected the *second* option more often, you are more of a *mother* to them.

1. Much can be learned from the lives of Ruth and Naomi. In light of their examples, what role must the *younger* generation—the Ruths—play in connecting with the older generation? Who are you connecting with who is younger?

   _____

   _____

   _____

   _____

   _____

   _____

2. What part must the *older* women—the Naomis—play in connecting with the younger women? Who are you connecting with who is older?

   _____

   _____

   _____

   _____

3. Think about some of the world's most famous **bridges**: London Bridge, Brooklyn Bridge and California's Golden Gate Bridge. Name some of the practical purposes, or functions, of a bridge and share how they apply to you being a "bridge" between generations.

Some practical functions of a bridge are...	Spiritually, this *function* represents...
_____	_____
_____	_____
_____	_____
_____	_____

"I cannot forget my mother. [S]he is my bridge. When I needed to get across,
she steadied herself long enough for me to run across safely."

~Renita Weems[1]

Connecting

"When the older women connect with the younger, there is a restoration of inheritance and legacy… I believe that God is connecting the Naomis and the Ruths and the sons of promise in these last days. We need to decide how we are going to position the next generations. I believe we need both age groups—the young and the old—if we're going to experience this restoration."

[adapted from Lisa's special session]

4. Share some personal *rewards* of raising your children—what did you impart into their lives? Why would you not trade the experience?

----

5. Proverbs 13:22 says that "Good people leave an inheritance to their grand-children, but the sinner's wealth passes to the godly." It's true that money is a part of this *inheritance*, but what other things are included? What kind of things did your grandparents or parents leave you?

Your **PART**

"We are the ones who choose what the next generation will inherit. Our children, whether born of the heart or of the body, will inherit one of two things: God's promises, or our fears. There is no neutral ground for any of us. Each and every generation of women is given the gift of time and influence. How will we choose to spend it on the daughters now before us?"

[page 125]

6. What are you passing on to your children? What will they inherit? Will it be your fears? Will it be sad stories of despair, difficulty and hopelessness? Or will it be an image of a faithful heavenly Father who somehow, someway always comes through—regardless of the circumstances? Take to heart and put into practice the instruction found in Psalm 78:1-8.

_____

_____

_____

_____

_____

_____

7. Elizabeth and Mary were two *ordinary* women who were used by God in *extraordinary* ways. However, they had to overcome some very difficult personal and cultural obstacles. List a few of them in the space below and then list some of the obstacles that God has empowered, or is empowering, you to overcome.

Elizabeth & Mary's Obstacles	My Obstacles—Past or Present
_____	_____
_____	_____
_____	_____
_____	_____
_____	_____

8. In God's eyes, Zechariah and Elizabeth were blameless, yet some people probably thought they had committed some secret sin because they were childless. Have others ever been suspicious or critical of you because of the hardships you were experiencing? If so, explain. Have *you* ever misjudged someone for a similar reason? If so, how?

_____

_____

_____

_____

_____

_____

9. When Gabriel appeared to Mary and gave her the news that she was chosen to bring forth the Messiah, why do you think he shared the news of Elizabeth's pregnancy with her? What can you learn from Mary's response to Gabriel in Luke 1:38?

_____

_____

_____

_____

Your PART

"What did Mary do with this amazing news? She ran to Elizabeth. The highly favored daughter sought the company of a consecrated grandmother and a beautiful interchange occurred. …Elizabeth did what women who are filled with the Holy Spirit are meant to do: she blessed (see Luke 1:42-45). In her words we find the blessing mothers and grandmothers should release over the daughters of God: Blessed is *she* who believes that what the Lord has said *to her* will be accomplished. Daughter, what has God said to you? Make it personal and believe it."

[adapted from pages 155, 156]

May the God of your hope so fill you with all *joy* and *peace* **in believing** [through the experience of your faith] that by the power of the Holy Spirit you may abound and be overflowing (bubbling over) with hope.

~Romans 15:13 AMP
[Italics and bold added for emphasis.]

10. What dream, vision or promise has God impregnated you with? What's in your heart that appears impossible but you can't seem to break free from? Read Habakkuk 2:2-3 and follow God's instruction to *write the vision*.

The dream, vision or promise God has given to me is:

_____

_____

_____

_____

11. After receiving God's promise through the angel Gabriel, both Zechariah and Mary questioned him as to *how* it would happen. Have you questioned God as to how His promise to you would take place? What obstacle(s) of impossibility can you not seem to get past?

_____

_____

_____

_____

_____

Planting PRINCIPLE

"Fear must always first be confronted before any promise of heaven can be heard on earth. If you are captive to fear, you cannot truly hear or bear what God is about to say. Instead of listening and allowing God's message to enlarge your life, you are too overwhelmed by trying to figure out how it will happen and what it will look like, and compiling a list of reasons why you can't do it. In that frame of mind, it is impossible to just open up and experience the wonder of it all. I don't know what God's dropped into your heart or told you, or what other people have told you. But I hear the Holy Spirit saying, 'Daughter, don't be afraid. Don't be afraid of any promise of heaven being released on earth through your life.'"

[adapted from pages 142, 143 and Lisa's special session.]

Trust God from the bottom of your heart; don't try to figure out everything on your own. Listen for God's voice in everything you do, everywhere you go; he's the one who will keep you on track. Don't assume that you know it all. Run to God! Run from evil!
~Proverbs 3:5-7 The Message

12. Have you ever resisted or opposed what God was saying to you? What did you learn through the situation?

_____

_____

_____

_____

_____

_____

_____

_____

_____

_____

_____

_____

13. Just as God seemed to be silent during the 400 years between the Old and New Testament, there are also times in our lives when He seems to be silent. Have you ever experienced a time like this? If so, describe the situation and how you responded. What is the *best* way to respond when God seems to be silent?

_____

_____

_____

_____

𝒴*our* **PART**

"Whenever God begins to do something big on Earth, He uses individuals who are willing to let Him get intimately involved in their lives. God is looking for people who will say, 'Lord, I am going to allow my personal prayers to become your vehicle for whatever you want.'"

[adapted from Lisa's special session and page 143]

"For the eyes of the Lord run to and fro throughout the whole earth to show Himself strong in behalf of those whose hearts are blameless toward Him…"

~**2 Chronicles 16:9 AMP**

14. Are you available and willing to allow God's Spirit to pray through you—to be an instrument through which His kingdom can come and His will be done on earth as it is in heaven?

_____

_____

_____

_____

15. For many years Zechariah and Elizabeth cried out to God for the legacy of a son. By sending them John (the Baptist), God not only answered *their* prayers, but also the prayers of countless others. What are you crying out to God for? What can you expect Him to do in your situation? (Check out Ephesians 3:20.)

_____

_____

_____

I have set watchmen upon your walls, O Jerusalem,
who will never hold their peace day or night;
you who [are His servants and by your prayers] **put the Lord
in remembrance [of His promises]**, keep not silence.
~Isaiah 62:6 AMP
[Boldness added for emphasis.]

16. Prayer is a powerful two-way conversation with the Master of all creation—it opens a portal that allows the power of heaven to invade earth. According to Isaiah 62:6, God wants us to remind Him of His promises—to respectfully repeat to Him what He spoke to us in our hearts and through His Word. Read Jeremiah 1:12 and Numbers 23:19 and write down what these Scriptures say to you about God and His faithfulness to keep His Word.

_____

_____

_____

_____

_____

_____

_____

_____

_____

_____

_____

_____

_____

Planting PRINCIPLE

"You may never know what is actually in your personal prayer until it is answered. A prayer for a son or a daughter may be about a whole lot more than your having a child. Your prayer for a lost loved one may be a whole lot bigger than that person's not going to hell. Your business' success may have a whole lot more to do than you know with heaven's purpose. …When we draw near and are honest, God can turn around our issues and then take what blesses and heals us on an individual basis and magnify it for the healing of many—sometimes even for the healing of nations."

[adapted from pages 144, 145]

…The earnest (heartfelt, continued) prayer of a righteous man makes tremendous power available [dynamic in its working] (AMP). Elijah, for instance, human just like us, prayed hard that it wouldn't rain, and it didn't—not a drop for three and a half years. Then he prayed that it would rain, and it did. The showers came and everything started growing again (The Message).
~James 5:16-18

Release a Blessing!

"What is this 'blessing,' this important act that no one can live well without?
Here's one way to explain it: 'words and actions that provide an indelible picture
of affirmation in a person's mind and memory.' To bless is to honor, praise, salute.
To be blessed is to be given power for success, prosperity, and longevity."

~**Gary Smalley & John Trent, Ph.D.**[2]
[Italics added for emphasis.]

Put It in Writing

Do you have a biological or adopted daughter or granddaughter? How about a younger woman at church, in your neighborhood, or at work who looks up to you? This precious princess of the King would greatly benefit from a letter of encouragement from you. This is one proven way to release a blessing into her life. The truth is, your words carry a lot of weight in her life and can have an indelible impact on her for all eternity. Block out at least 30 minutes of time to totally focus on this daughter of promise and write her a letter.

Include Words of Value

You don't have to be a seasoned writer—just share your heart. Focus on her positive qualities. Whatever her strengths are, write them down and tell her how much you admire her. Be her cheerleader. Express your desire for her to do great works—even greater than what you've done. Expose any fear or weakness of yours that you don't want to see duplicated in her life, giving her Scriptures to confront and defeat the enemy. You may want to conclude your letter with a *prayer of blessing* over her, filled with Scriptures and words that paint a powerful portrait of success.

Deliver It Creatively

Be creative. You can type or handwrite your letter on colorful paper or parchment. You can even place it in a frame. If your relationship with her is not very close, you may want to just mail it. However, if your relationship is vibrant and strong, it may make more of an impact on her if you give it to her personally. You can take her to her favorite restaurant or have her over to your home for tea or coffee.

Pray and ask the Lord to lead you in this activity. He intimately knows the person you are writing the letter for, and therefore knows what words to use and how to deliver it in the way that will touch her the greatest.

This activity can be modified and applied to any daughter of God.

> Therefore encourage (admonish, exhort) one another and edify
> (strengthen and build up) one another, just as you are doing.
> **~1 Thessalonians 5:11 AMP**

Making Connections

> Grandparents are proud of their grandchildren, and
> children should be proud of their parents.
> **~Proverbs 17:6 CEV**

Grandparents Are Special
by Ruth Bell Graham

Although we were deprived of our natural grandparents while growing up in China, the senior missionaries were like our own grandparents—Uncle Jimmie and Aunt Sophie Graham, Dr. and Mrs. Woods, Grandma and Grandpa Reynolds, and others.

In the Orient, age was respected because it implied the accumulation of wisdom that the years bring. To have a grandparent in the home was considered a privilege rather than a burden.

…Our children did not get to see as much of Bill's parents as we would have liked. They lived in Charlotte. But the children were deeply influenced by their paternal grandparents because of their kindly and godly lives. Fortunately we lived much closer to my parents. Living across the road from them was one of the nicest things that ever happened to our first four children. (Ned was born after the move up the mountain.)

They were ideal grandparents—strict disciplinarians but full of love and fun.

Many nights the girls would spend with their grandparents. I can still see them, like three little stairsteps, dressed for bed and hugging their favorite blankets or pillows, as they climbed our curving drive and walked the short distance across the road to Daddy's and Mother's.

Those evenings were always family times, as they had been in China. Games to be played, books to be read aloud. Mother made clothes for their dolls, nursed them when they were sick, let them help her work in her flowers in the spring and rake leaves in the fall and lick the pan after making a batch of fudge.

Since Daddy was a doctor, whenever medication or stitches were needed, he was available.

Both were great storytellers. They were happy Christians. They were part of God's special provision for us during the many occasions Bill was away on crusades. Just as Jesus promised, "He who leaves family for My sake and the Gospel's shall receive a hundredfold in this life" (see Mark 10:29, 30).

Those of you who have not had a loving Christian heritage can make sure your children have one. Even if you feel it is too late, commit the wasted years and lost opportunities to God. Love each one who comes to mind, and pray.

Then, look around for some young person you can encourage and help along the way.

Edited from Ruth Bell Graham's *Blessings for a Mother's Day* (Word Publishing, Nashville, TN 2001) pp. 115-118.

Write YOUR LIFE

Have you ever been considered *insignificant* and, consequently, overlooked or left behind by others? God doesn't see you that way. To Him you are priceless! And He views the women around you in the same way. He has *great* things planned for your life and theirs. This is the season to unite and overcome the obstacles of fear and failure—to encourage the gift of God in yourself and others and embrace the impossible dreams God has deposited in you. What is His Spirit speaking to you through this special session? What adjustments is He asking you to make?

> ### *Planting* PRINCIPLE
>
> "I believe there is a generation of older women living right now who are saying, 'We've started our lives full and we are at the end of our seasons and we feel empty. We have nothing to bring, nothing to give.' But that is a lie. The older women can teach women my age and younger to glean what has been left behind. There is sustenance in what has been left behind."
> [adapted from Lisa's special session]

1. Quotations About *Mothers*, The Quote Garden (http://www.quotegarden.com/mothers.html, retrieved 6/4/08).
2. Gary Smalley & John Trent, Ph.D., *The Blessing Workbook* (Thomas Nelson Publishers, Nashville, TN 1993) p.20.

notes from special session

Home is Where There is One to Love Us
by Charles Swain

Home's not merely four square walls,
Though with pictures hung and gilded;
Home is where Affection calls—
Filled with shrines the Hearth had builded!
Home! Go watch the faithful dove,
Sailing 'neath the heaven above us.
Home is where there's one to love!
Home is where there's one to love us!

Home's not merely roof and room,
It needs something to endear it;
Home is where the heart can bloom,
Where there's some kind lip to cheer it!
What is home with none to meet,
None to welcome, none to greet us?
Home is sweet, and only sweet,
Where there's one we love to meet us!

*Our homes provide a cozy place away from the world where we love
and are loved. It's fun to be out with our friends playing and going
places, but at the end of the day it's always good to come home.[1]*

I now realize that I am flourishing today because God has positioned me
under the nurturing care of a spiritual mother who was watching,
waiting and believing in me. Even if it's something you've never
had for yourself, it is available and attainable for every woman.
~C.Y., CO

Creating the
Environment of Nurture

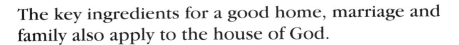

Read chapters 9 and 10 in the *Nurture* book and view DVD session 4.

The key ingredients for a good home, marriage and family also apply to the house of God.

environment
The conditions that surround people and affect the way they live.[2]

1. Part of creating an environment of nurture includes creating an atmosphere of *warmth*. In what specific ways did your parents (or other homes you visited) express warmth as you were growing up? How do you express warmth to your husband and children? Is there anything your parents did that communicated coldness to you as a child that you wish to avoid repeating? What was it?

Planting
PRINCIPLE

"Environment and atmospheres can work for or against the fostering of nurture. …If life is to flourish, it must have warmth… …warmth can be cultivated in more than outward ways. Warmth can be conveyed in a smile, a touch, a gift, a meal eaten together, and the beauty of our environment. Emotional warmth is an integral part of *nurture*."

[adapted from pages 183, 186, 187]

2. Rituals are also important. These simple routines and traditions help connect your family and shape its overall direction. What rituals can you remember from your childhood days that were a positive source of peace, safety, comfort, enjoyment and warmth? What rituals have you established for *your* children and family?

    Growing up, the rituals I remember enjoying most were...

    _____

    _____

    _____

    _____

    Some of the rituals I/we have established for my/our children and family are...

Daily/Nightly	Weekly/Monthly	Seasonally/Yearly
_____	_____	_____
_____	_____	_____
_____	_____	_____
_____	_____	_____

> "A mother is the truest friend we have, when trials heavy and sudden, fall upon us; when adversity takes the place of prosperity; when friends who rejoice with us in our sunshine desert us; when trouble thickens around us, still will she cling to us, and endeavor by her kind precepts and counsels to dissipate the clouds of darkness, and cause peace to return to our hearts."
> ~Washington Irving[3]

Locating Yourself

FOOD FOR THOUGHT

Having an ample supply of good food that's fun to eat is another powerful part of creating an environment of nurture. How does food factor in at your house?

1. Do you eat with the TV *on* or *off* the majority of the time?

    _____

2. How many meals a week do you eat *together* around the table?

    _____

3. Which word more often describes mealtime at your house—*energizing* or *exhausting*?

_____

4. What is more commonly heard during dinner—*conversation and laughter* or *silence*?

_____

5. Are mealtimes something you and your children *like* or *loathe* to share with others?

_____

_____

_____

> The answers to these questions are definitely food for thought. Ask the Lord to show you what needs to change around the dinner table at your home, and ask Him for the strength to do it. (Check out Isaiah 40:28-31.)

3. The miraculous medicine of laughter is also a key ingredient to creating an atmosphere of nurture. What type of *clean* sayings, stories or e-mails make you and your family laugh? What kind of cartoons and movies make you giggle the most?

_____

_____

_____

_____

Have a heaping helping of these funnies on hand and allow the light-hearted laughter to contagiously fly free in your family whenever you can!

Laugh! It's an Energizing Exercise!

"As with aerobic exercise, laughter temporarily accelerates the heart rate, increases blood pressure and breathing, enlarges circulation and enhances the flow of oxygen in and out of the body. A hearty belly laugh also exercises the upper torso, lungs, heart, shoulders, arms, abdomen, diaphragm and legs. Laughing 100 to 200 times a day is equivalent to ten minutes of rowing or jogging. …Belly laughter is the most therapeutic form of laughter, and that is the reason I recommend ten belly laughs a day to all of my patients. Ten belly laughs are roughly equivalent to thirty minutes of aerobic exercise."

~Don Colbert, M.D.[4]

A happy heart is good medicine and a cheerful mind works healing,
but a broken spirit dries up the bones.
~Proverbs 17:22 AMP

4. How is the environment of nurture in your church? In what practical ways does your church's women's ministry provide a good atmosphere for nurture? What areas do you feel could use improvement?

    _____

    _____

    _____

    _____

Pray for your women's ministry and its leaders. Don't just grumble and complain to others behind the scene. Ask God to give you creative ideas to be a part of the solution.

Planting
PRINCIPLE

"...it is never becoming for anyone, least of all Christian women, to be rude. Being a daughter of heaven does not give you a license to be rude on earth. We are not some elite group of forgiven snobs...we are earth's servants. If anything we have to be kinder, gentler, and politer than any other daughters who walk the earth. ...We are not merely representing ourselves to the world around us, we represent the kingdom of heaven and the cause of Christ [see 2 Corinthians 5:19-20]. It is completely inappropriate for us to behave in a rude or ignorant manner."
[pages 196, 197, 198]
[Scripture added for emphasis.]

5. Why are manners such an important part of nurture? What is the basis for good manners and what do they actually reveal about us? How does it make you feel when someone is rude or impatient with you?

    _____

    _____

    _____

    _____

    _____

    _____

    _____

    _____

    _____

    _____

    _____

6. *Etiquette* is basically the noble [polite and gracious] approach to the course of life—it is the language of manners. Briefly describe and give an example of *introduction* and *restaurant* etiquette.

_____
_____
_____
_____
_____
_____
_____
_____
_____
_____

Take the Challenge!
Is your etiquette up to par? Have some fun and learn at the same time by taking these online quizzes on manners and etiquette. Visit http://northeastetiquette.com/quiz.html and http://uktv.co.uk/style/quiz/aid/565150/.

> Similarly, teach the older women to live in a way that honors God.
> They must not slander others or be heavy drinkers. Instead, they should
> teach others what is good. These older women must train the younger
> women to love their husbands and their children, to live wisely and
> be pure, to work in their homes, to do good, and to be submissive
> to their husbands. Then they will not bring shame on the word of God.
> **~Titus 2:3-5 NLT vs.2**

7. Part of God's divine design is for younger women to learn from the older women how to create an environment of nurture in their home and relationships. Slowly read Titus 2:3-5 and list the seven things older women are instructed to train the younger women to do.

1. _____
2. _____
3. _____
4. _____
5. _____
6. _____
7. _____

8. Loving your husband is a top priority in God's book. Do you know what your husband's *love language* is? From his point of view, what things say to him that you love him? Are you speaking his language, or are you loving him the way you want to be loved?

_____

_____

_____

_____

Discover Your Spouse's Love Language

Ask your husband to carefully read through these five statements and select the one that *best* sums up the way he feels especially loved. His number one answer is his *primary* love language. The next strongest way he feels loved is his secondary love language. Take the quiz yourself and find *your* primary and secondary love languages.

_____ 1. I feel especially loved when people express how grateful they are for me, and for the simple, everyday things I do.

_____ 2. I feel especially loved when a person gives me undivided attention and spends time alone with me.

_____ 3. I feel especially loved by someone who brings me gifts and other tangible expressions of love.

_____ 4. I feel especially loved when someone pitches in to help me, perhaps by running errands or taking on my household chores.

_____ 5. I feel especially loved when a person expresses feelings for me through physical contact.

Love Language Key: 1. Words of Affirmation 2. Quality Time 3. Gifts 4. Acts of Service 5. Physical Touch

Your husband's primary love language is _____.
His secondary love language is _____.

Your primary love language is _____.
Your secondary love language is _____.

This information is adapted from Dr. Gary Chapman's 30-second Love Language Quiz, http://www.fivelovelanguages.com/learn.html.

Recommended Reading
The Five Love Languages: How to Express Heartfelt Commitment to Your Mate, by Dr. Gary Chapman (Northfield Publishing, Chicago, IL, 1995).

Your PART

"Men, like all of us, deserve to be loved the way they can hear it. So if your husband loves to be talked about, talk about him. Tell him how godly he is. Don't point out all of his faults. You'll build him up by giving strength to his strengths."

[adapted from session 4]

---

9. One way to express love to your husband is by *submitting* to him. Although some would prefer to remove this God-ordained instruction from Scripture, it is, nevertheless, vital to enabling women to truly flourish as God intended. Briefly describe what submission *is* and what it *is not*. What is the Holy Spirit speaking to you about this area of your life?

    _____

    _____

    _____

    _____

10. Each of your children and grandchildren also has their own love language. It may be hearing caring words, receiving a tender touch, getting a small gift, going to a special place, or a combination of things. Write each of their names in the spaces provided and briefly describe the things you have noticed communicate to them that they are loved, valued and have purpose.

Child/Grandchild's Name	Love Language
_____	_____
_____	_____
_____	_____
_____	_____
_____	_____

    Note: If you don't really know your child's love language, ask God to help you learn it. Become a student of how they respond to the time and attention you give them. Seek to understand what actions from you (and others) make them *come alive* and *thrive* as a person. Then begin to speak their love language. You will both be glad you did!

11. Training your children properly is very important to their development and use-fulness in God's kingdom. As you read through the chapter on training and listened to session 4, what things regarding discipline really stood out to you? What truths regarding the consequences of *not* disciplining your children did the Holy Spirit make real to you?

_____

_____

_____

_____

_____

_____

> Train up a child in the way he should go [and in keeping with his individual gift or bent], and when he is old he will not depart from it.
> **~Proverbs 22:6 AMP**

Pruning

"You need to let your kids get involved with some of the stuff so that you can be involved with some of the 'God things.' And then you need to weigh what's really important and what's not really important. Kids don't really remember if everything was perfectly clean in the house or not; they remember whether they felt comfortable in the house."

[session 4]

What tasks do you need to prune from your plate and delegate to your kids? In order for you to move from barely surviving as a parent to actually thriving, ask God to show you what to let go of and to give you and your children the strength you need to walk it out.

12. Everyone's life is influencing somebody, and through our influence we are training others. Is your sphere of influence *greater* than or *less* than it was at this time a year ago? How has it changed, and what do you think has affected it?

_____

_____

_____

_____

13. What lesson(s) in life did you learn the hard way that you would rather not see your daughter or daughter of God have to go through?

_____

_____

_____

_____

He who heeds instruction and correction
is [not only himself] in the way of life
[but also] **is a way of life for others**.
And he who neglects or refuses
reproof [not only himself] goes astray
[but also] causes to err and is
a path toward ruin for others.
~Proverbs 10:17 AMP
[Boldness added for emphasis.]

Planting
PRINCIPLE

"We're being watched whether we want to be watched or not. We're being watched by the world…and we're being watched by the daughters. The younger girls are not watching for you to fail—they are watching for you to succeed."
[adapted from session 4]

14. What does it mean to *live wisely*? What kinds of things should you, as a wise woman, let go of and what things should you hold onto?

_____

_____

_____

_____

_____

15. Are you looking for direction or advice on what to do as a wife or mother? Always go to God first and then seek the counsel of a seasoned Christian woman—one who *models* what you want to be and lives the way you want to live. Take a few moments and make a list of the qualities you want as a wife, mother and woman of God. Pray and ask the Lord to create a divine connection with women who fit this description.

_____

_____

_____

_____

Connecting

"We are women who walk through an earthly life made up of seasons. Beauty and strength are to be found in each and every season, but we face vulnerability and weakness when we try to skip one season to enter another. Our strength similarly weakens if we strain for what is passed and neglect to give attention to what is before us. Seasoned women empower others to find their way."

[page 176]

Remember, as you reach out to receive help from someone older and more mature, someone younger than you is probably looking for guidance too. Be willing, open and available to help the daughter(s) your heavenly Father brings across your path.

"The sweetest sounds to mortals given are heard in *mother, home* and *heaven*."
~William Goldsmith Brown[5]
[Italics added for emphasis.]

"The Survey Says...!"

One of the best ways for a company to improve its overall productivity and approval rating in the eyes of the public is to take a survey from its customers. Similarly, you can learn a lot about the environment of nurture in your home by getting some open and honest feedback from your family. Just the fact that you sincerely want to know their opinion will go a long way in building bridges of love and unity where strife may presently exist.

Take time to sit with your husband and each of your children and ask them the questions below. Record each person's response on a separate sheet of paper.

1. What are your top 3 favorite foods?
2. What are your 2 *least* favorite foods?
3. If you could change 1 thing about our home, what would it be?
4. What are your 3 favorite rituals (traditions/routines) that we do as a family/couple? Why?

5. Complete this sentence: I enjoy (or *don't* enjoy) inviting people to our house because ...
6. Complete this sentence: I know my wife/mom really loves me when she ...
7. Complete this sentence: It's hard for me to know my wife/mom loves me when she ...

Note: More than one response should be encouraged and received even if not indicated in the question.

Remember: This is *not* the time to start a *family feud* and get defensive about the answers each person gives—it's time to hear their hearts and prayerfully discover what you can do to improve the overall atmosphere of nurture in your home. Take their responses to the Lord in prayer and ask Him to show you what to do. Then, if you're married, go to your husband and, together, carefully review each person's answers. Pray and ask the Lord to show you both how to *maximize* the positive and *minimize* the negative by making Spirit-led changes.

The changes I/we feel like God is showing me/us to make are ...

_____

_____

_____

_____

_____

_____

_____

_____

_____

_____

_____

_____

_____

_____

_____

A wise woman builds her house; a foolish woman
tears hers down with her own hands.
~Proverbs 14:1 NLT

"Nothing changes until one generation of women rises up beyond what they have known and seen and makes the declaration, no matter the cost, 'There must be change! I will stand in the gap. It no longer matters what I had or did not have in my life. I want something more for the daughters who now surround me. I want something more for my friends who live in perpetual pain. I want to love well and teach others to love and be well loved.'"

[page 164]

Will you dare to be different and do whatever it takes to create an environment of nurture at home and wherever you go? Your Father in heaven stands ready to use you as an instrument of change in the earth! Pray and ask Him to give you a passion for the young daughters coming up and to show you how you can bring solutions to the world around you. Write what He speaks to your heart.

_____

_____

_____

_____

_____

_____

_____

_____

_____

_____

_____

_____

_____

_____

_____

_____

_____

_____

_____

Things a hardy laugh can do!
- Reduce stress levels
- Lower blood pressure
- Elevate your mood
- Boost your immune system
- Improve brain functioning
- Protect your heart
- Connect you with others
- Promote instant relaxation
- Make you feel good

This information is adapted and taken from Dr. Don Colbert's book *Stress Less* (Nashville, TN Thomas Nelson Inc. 2005).

1. *Everyday Graces – A Child's Book of Good Manners*, Edited, with commentary, by Karen Santorum (ISI Books: Wilmington, DE, 2003) p. 41. 2. Lisa Bevere, *Nurture* (Faith Words, New York, NY 2008) p. 183. 3. Quotations About Mothers, The Quote Garden (http://www.quotegarden.com/mothers.html, retrieved 5/24/08). 4. "The Miraculous Medicine of Laughter," Don Colbert, M.D. (*Enjoying Everyday Life* magazine, November 2005, Joyce Meyer Ministries, Inc., Fenton, MO) p.22. 5. See note 3.

notes from session 4

I just finished reading *Nurture*… I can hardly see through my tears. I am on the board of an international organization that is on the frontlines of human trafficking and prostitution located in Thailand. This was more than a gift; it has compelled me to move forward on some rather large jobs God has called me to! I am filled with a God-sized awe in knowing that what I have been called to is being shared by countless other daughters around the world!! Thank you!

~K. G., CO

The Response of Nurture 5

Read chapter 11 in the *Nurture* book and view DVD session 5.

Birthing a Heart of Compassion

Locating Yourself

DO I HAVE A *COMPASSIONATE* HEART OF NURTURE?
Choose the way you are most likely to respond in each situation below.

1. When I see a poor man at an intersection with a sign asking for help, I …
   a. Turn the other way and try to ignore him.
   b. Think briefly about giving him money, but decide he'll use it for the wrong reason.
   c. Pray and ask God what He would have me do in the situation.

2. When I hear of the number of babies who have been aborted since *Roe vs. Wade*, I …
   a. Really don't think too much about it.
   b. Get aggravated, but quickly conclude that there is really nothing I can do about it.
   c. Am deeply grieved and moved to pray and ask God how I can help save innocent lives.

3. When images of starving children flash across my TV screen, I …
   a. Quickly reach for the remote to turn the channel.
   b. Am saddened by what I see, but doubt the money I might send would actually get to the children.
   c. Pray for the children and parents and ask God to show me if this is a trustworthy ministry to the poor and starving that I can support.

4. When I learn of a widow neighbor having a lack of food because she's short of money, I ...

  a. Say it's a shame and quickly put the blame on the government and her family for not helping.

  b. Want to help, but I'm afraid I won't have enough for my family, *or* I think helping may offend her.

  c. Pray for her and try to build a relational bridge to her to learn the best ways I can help.

GRADE: Which letter option did you circle most? If you circled mostly...

As: You have room to grow in the area of compassion.

Bs: Your heart of compassion is developing and will enlarge more as you let the Lord heal you of past hurts.

Cs: You have a heart of compassion that's open to the promptings of God's Spirit. Stay tuned in to Him.

c o m p a s s i o n
A suffering with another; painful sympathy; a sensation of sorrow excited by the distress of misfortunes of another; pity.[1]

Planting PRINCIPLE

"Women bring such the heart of compassion to the table... I've always been touched by the poor and the needy, but I didn't know how to move beyond just being touched to being a solution to it. And I believe that all of you are here to bring solutions to this. We need women who won't just cry—we need women who will cry out and will weep and wail for something to change. I want to position you with compassion because compassion is the response of nurture."

[adapted from session 5]

1. Describe the differences between *whining* and *wailing*. What happens inside of you when you wail? Describe one of the most memorable moments in your life when you wailed and what it was about.

_____
_____
_____
_____
_____
_____
_____
_____
_____
_____
_____

2. If you have never really wailed, what do you think it will take to birth a wail in you? Pray and ask the Father to allow you to *see* and *hear* what is necessary to awaken the compassionate heart of Christ in you.

_____

_____

_____

_____

_____

_____

_____

Your PART

"Before those first two wails, I lived in myself. I lived in what I could control, what I could manage, and in parameters that didn't make my friends uncomfortable… You know, sometimes when you start doing stuff for God, it makes your friends uncomfortable. You have to understand, God will push you out of your comfort zone on every single level so that this world will be comforted."

[adapted from session 5]

Ask yourself some soul-searching questions: "Who really calls the shots in my life? Do I live within the safety of the 'box' I have created, or is my life truly surrendered? Am I more concerned about pleasing people than pleasing God?" Get quiet before the Lord; ask Him for the strength and desire to face and defeat your fears and the power to live your life truly yielded to Him.

3. How has the Father pushed you out of your *comfort zone*? What has He asked (or led) you to do that you did not, and probably would not, choose to do on your own? How has it become a blessing in disguise and *enlarged* your life?

_____

_____

_____

_____

_____

_____

4. Pause a few moments to take an inventory of your commitments: Where are you regularly investing the resources of your *time, talent* and/or *treasure* in the lives of others? What "bigger" thing(s) are you tied to that help you live outside of yourself?

_____

_____

_____

_____

_____

Please know that God doesn't want you to be *over*-committed and spread so thin that you are lacking provision for you and your family. But, He does want you involved some-where. As you seek Him and stay in relationship with Him, He'll make that *somewhere* crystal clear and show you how and what to give. **Check out** Psalm 25 for a few of His promises to direct your path.

Positioning Yourself
"My life got enlarged when I tied it to something bigger than my little world, with my little limits, and my little budget. I was no longer just a stay-at-home mom with three children under five—I was a woman solving world crisis. And we really need to see it that way. I believe women have the ability over the next decade or two to solve the crisis of poverty, the widow and the orphan. I believe we are the ones who will open our arms and stretch forth to the poor and the needy. But we need to be positioned to do this."

[adapted from session 5]

In what practical ways can you position yourself and your family to become part of the solution to the crisis of poverty, the widow and the orphan? What outreach(es) in your church or area can you begin to invest in? Is there a food bank, community center, pregnancy center, or other ministry you can help? Get quiet and ask the Lord to confirm His will for you. Remember, He always leads by peace—not pressure (see Colossians 3:15).

Religion that God our Father accepts as pure and faultless is this:
to look after orphans and widows in their distress
and to keep oneself from being polluted by the world.
~James 1:27 NIV

5. Read Ezekiel 16:49-50. What was the *root* sin of Sodom? How do you see this sin being committed in America today? What can you do to help change it?

_____

_____

_____

_____

6. Has God ever placed a desire, or hunger, in your heart to go somewhere and help someone else *before* you were actually asked? Describe the situation and the door of opportunity that He eventually opened.

_____

_____

_____

_____

But if anyone has this world's goods (resources for sustaining life) and sees his brother and fellow believer in need, yet closes his heart of compassion against him, how can the love of God live and remain in him?
~1 John 3:17 AMP

Planting PRINCIPLE

"Each one of us has a circle of influence in our world and during our short season on this earth, we possess the power to effect change. We live in a world that is hurting, but we steward an answer. This earth is full to overflowing with needs and pain. But there are just as many ways and individuals crafted to meet and heal them. Your giving and serving may start small, but they will always end up with an impact that is big if you are consistent."
[page 213]

7. It is very important that we respond and give to others for the *right* reasons. For what reason should we *always* give to others? For what reason should we *never* feel compelled to give? When we give, who are we ultimately giving to? (Check out Proverbs 19:17.)

_____

_____

_____

_____

_____

_____

8. Romans 12:6 declares, "God has given each of us the ability to do certain things well" (TLB). What specific gifts and talents has God entrusted to you? *How* and *where* in your sphere of influence are you using them?

    _____

    _____

    _____

    _____

    _____

9. Is there a talent that you have *buried* and chosen not to use because of fear? If so, what is it and what are you afraid of? Get quiet and ask the Lord to show you your heart and how to confront and conquer the fear.

    _____

    _____

    _____

    _____

    _____

Pruning

"Understand that fear will ultimately make you do things you would never dream of doing, say things you would never dream of saying, listen to things you should never give ear to. Fear will cause you to view things in such a twisted manner that you lose all healthy sense of perspective. Then you will doubt what you should trust and trust what you should doubt."

[pages 219, 220]

The list of phobias, or fears, that plague people is seemingly endless. What fears are plaguing you and hindering you from experiencing the abundant life Jesus promised (see John 10:10)? Are you ready to seek the Lord and allow Him to reveal and prune the root fears that are holding you hostage? He stands ready, willing and able to help!

I prayed to the Lord, and he answered me, freeing me from all my fears.
Those who look to him for help will be radiant with joy;
no shadow of shame will darken their faces.
~Psalm 34:4-5 NLT

10. Read the parable of the talents in Matthew 25:14-30. What do verses 24-30 say to you about the *unfaithful* servant's character and his relationship with his master? Are there any qualities in him that you see in yourself that you want God to remove? If so, what are they?

_____

_____

_____

_____

_____

_____

_____

11. What happens when you see hardship in the world—do you *shut down* because of discouragement and fear, or do you feel *challenged* and *motivated* to get involved? Pray and ask the Lord to show you why you respond the way you do. Write what He reveals.

_____

_____

_____

_____

_____

_____

_____

Are You a *Channel* or a *Reservoir*?

"One of the main reasons why God wants to bless and prosper us is so that we can bless others. He doesn't want us to be like a water *reservoir* that just collects; after time, stagnant water usually stinks. He wants to use us as a *channel* to allow His blessings to flow through us to others. A channel is an instrument or place where things flow through. The water flowing through a channel is usually fresh, clean, and pure. When we receive things from God and then at His prompting give them to others, our lives become like a flowing channel of water—fresh, clean, and pure. …God wants us to enjoy the things we have but hold them loosely. You and I had nothing when we came into this world, and we'll have nothing when we leave it. When we act as a channel, always ready to pass something on to others, God will see to it that we always have a fresh supply of whatever we need."

~Joyce Meyer[2]
[Italics added for emphasis.]

12. What does it mean to "take notice" of something in the Spirit? What happens if you *resist* the promptings and impressions of God's Spirit and do not act? What happens when you *obey* them?

_____

_____

_____

_____

_____

13. Is there a ministry or relief organization you "accidentally" discovered that really grabbed hold of your heart, but you dismissed getting involved with it? What ministry is it? Have you come across it more than once? What is the Holy Spirit speaking to you about partnering with them or investing in the work they are doing?

Planting
PRINCIPLE

"There is a special reward reserved for us when we exhibit child-of-God-type behavior. God is a giver and so likewise we should give. We are each blessed to be a blessing. What comes to our hands becomes dusty and stagnant when it stops with us. Yes, some of the blessing is for us to keep, some is for us to multiply, some is for us to pass on, and some is to be given away—but all is ours only to steward. We are stewards of our gifts and talents, our resources, our children, our words—everything. There is ultimately no ownership for the daughter of God. He is the ultimate, final word on how we live our lives and spend our money."
[adapted from page 210 and session 5]

"'For I was hungry, and you fed me. I was thirsty, and you gave me a drink. I was a stranger, and you invited me into your home. I was naked, and you gave me clothing. I was sick, and you cared for me. I was in prison, and you visited me.'

Then these righteous ones will reply, 'Lord, when did we ever see you hungry and feed you? Or thirsty and give you something to drink? Or a stranger and show you hospitality? Or naked and give you clothing? When did we ever see you sick or in prison, and visit you?' And the King will tell them, 'I assure you, when you did it to one of the least of these my brothers and sisters, you were doing it to me!'"

~Matthew 25:35-40 NLT

Makin' a List...Checkin' It *MORE THAN* Twice!

Have you ever become prey for the inward predator of self-pity? Has your focus ever become so clouded that all you could seem to see was how bad *you* had it and how poor *you* were in comparison to others? I think all of us have experienced this at times.

To help you fight against this ferocious fiend that feeds the flesh, get a notebook or use some blank pages in the back of your Bible and make a list of the many wonderful ways God has blessed you. Can you breathe? Can you see? Are you able to walk? Do you have running water, clothes on your back, and food on your table? Then you have plenty to thank God for.

Take some time to meditate on what God has protected you from, how He has provided for your needs, and when He has showered you with mercy that you didn't deserve. As you slow down and reflect upon His goodness to you, the Holy Spirit will saturate your spirit and soul with a sweet satisfaction of gratitude and gratefulness that is sure to drive away the predator of self-pity.

I [will] recall the many miracles he did for me so long ago. Those wonderful deeds are constantly in my thoughts. I cannot stop thinking about them.

~Psalm 77:11-12 TLB
[Word in brackets found in other versions added for emphasis.]

Count Your Blessings...Name Them One by One!

_____

_____

_____

_____

_____

_____

Making Connections

Whatever your hand finds to do, do it with all your might…
~**Ecclesiastes 9:10 NIV**

Banchte Shekha: Women Helping Women in Bangladesh
by Jim Mullins and Alice Boatwright

It is dawn on a December morning in Bangladesh. The sun is rising in a luminous red ball over fields of yellow flowers. Chickens peck under tall banana trees, their leaves heavy with dew. A dog barks at the empty sky, and, in the distance, the call of Muslim prayer ripples along the cool, moist breeze.

Outside the bamboo huts, women fan breakfast fires. The rising smoke sways and mingles with clouds of fog that hang over tiny ponds.

Along the road is a sign, "Banchte Shekha: Development Program for Women and Children." A red arrow points across a small pond to a compound of bamboo build-ings where a group of women is gathering for breakfast. Banchte Shekha founder, An-gela Gomes—a vibrant woman in her early forties—laughs and chats with the women as she helps serve a meal of porridge, chapatis and papaya.

Many of these women have spent the night at Banchte Shekha—a safe haven for them from an abusive husband or in-laws. For others, Banchte Shekha, which is Bangla for "learning to live," is part of a longer journey toward dignity. For all of them, Banchte Shekha offers hope because one woman believed that poor village women could have better lives, even when they didn't believe it themselves.

In the small village Angela grew up in, she and other women worked hard, but were also beaten, disrespected and expected to marry young and "settle down." An-gela refused to accept this lifestyle and got into a mission school and began to work alongside the nuns and priest reaching out to the poor in the area.

Angela was determined to find an answer for the women. She began traveling to different villages to connect with women who shared in her heart for freedom. These women caught her vision and united with her to make a difference. This was the birth of Banchte Shekha, a place to help women learn to live.

Project after project, the women of Banchte Shekha steadily and persistently continued to labor for the freedom and value of the women. What started with only a few in 1981 exploded to 5,000 members in 1985 and today has more than 20,000 women shaping the Bangladeshi culture.

There is such power in women gathering together with purpose, united with one voice.

Excerpt and information taken from "Banchte Shekha: Women Helping Women in Bangladesh" story at http://www.jim-mullins.com/Bangladesh.html.

Whatever you do, work at it with all your heart,
as working for the Lord, not for men.
~Colossians 3:23 NIV

Write YOUR LIFE

After reading through the chapter and viewing session 5, God's Spirit is probably prompting you to do something. What specific actions is He asking you to take? What kind of compassion is He birthing in you? Keep in mind, you cannot out-give God!

"If you give, you will receive. Your gift will return to you in full measure, pressed down, shaken together to make room for more, and running over. Whatever measure you use in giving—large or small—it will be used to measure what is given back to you."
~Luke 6:38 NLT

> **Planting PRINCIPLE**
>
> "It is time for God's daughters to open their arms to the needy and extend assistance to the poor. Each of us can make a small difference and collectively the effect will be vast."
>
> [page 211]

---

1. *American Dictionary of the English Language*, Noah Webster's First Edition 1828 (Republished in facsimile edition by Foundation for American Christian Education, San Francisco, CA, thirteenth printing 2000). 2. "God's Plan for Abundant Prosperity," Joyce Meyer (*Life In The Word* magazine, April 2001, Fenton, MO, Joyce Meyer Ministries, Inc.) p.13.

notes from session 5

Run Well

Read chapter 12 in the *Nurture* book and view DVD session 6.

Connecting with God

Locating Yourself

HOW *CONNECTED* TO GOD AM I?

On a scale of 1 to 10—1 being "Never" and 10 being "Always"—circle the number that best answers each question.

1. When I wake up each day, the first thing I do is tell God "good morning" and thank Him for the rest He gave me.
   1 2 3 4 5 6 7 8 9 10

2. When I am faced with a difficult decision, the first person I turn to for wisdom is God.
   1 2 3 4 5 6 7 8 9 10

3. When tragedy strikes me or my family, the first person I run to is the Lord.
   1 2 3 4 5 6 7 8 9 10

4. When I feel the gentle prompting of the Holy Spirit to do or not do something, I quickly obey.
   1 2 3 4 5 6 7 8 9 10

5. When something good happens to me, the first thing I do is thank God for His blessings.
   1 2 3 4 5 6 7 8 9 10

> **GRADE:** Add up the total of all the numbers you circled. If the sum is…
>
> **40 to 50:** You are connected to God in a strong way and being in relationship with Him is top priority to you.
>
> **25 to 39:** You value your relationship with God, but you have room to strengthen your connection with Him.
>
> **10 to 24:** At present, your relationship with God is rather distant. Welcome Him; He longs to be invited into your life.

Planting PRINCIPLE

"Beautiful one, the hour is late. Some of you are tired, but it is not yet time to sleep. It is time to awake. There are captive daughters in every age bracket and it is time they were free. Most of us have spent far too much time in a position of slavery when we are in fact royalty. Royalty is amazing, but it does not worship itself. Royalty has power and influence to spend on the lives of other people. We need to unleash the gift of nurture in all captive women and lead them to live in their true inheritance."
[adapted from session 6 and page 224]

step one: **AWAKE**

To *cease from sleep or inaction*; to excite from a state resembling sleep.[1] This step includes repentance—asking God to forgive us and cleanse us from wrong and turn in the direction of right.

This is all the more urgent, for you know how late it is; time is running out. Wake up, for our salvation is nearer now than when we first believed. The night is almost gone; the day of salvation will soon be here...
~Romans 13:11-12 NLT vs.2

1. Waking up is the way we start each day in the natural and each new season in the spirit. The waking process includes *repentance*, which is to recognize the sin in our lives, ask God to forgive us and cleanse us from all impurity, and turn away from it (see 1 John 1:9). Are there any things the Holy Spirit is prompting you to repent from right now?

_____

_____

_____

_____

_____

2. Can you look back over your life and remember a pivotal point when you awakened and followed through on a commitment to do something that pushed you totally out of your comfort zone? Describe the situation.

_____

_____

_____

_____

_____

step two: **ARISE**

To rise from a quiet, inactive, or subjugated (under enemy control) state to become active or vocal; to change positions; to rise above and move beyond what has been into what will be.[2]

> "…Awake, O sleeper, rise up from the dead, and Christ will give you light."
> **~Ephesians 5:14**

3. When you wake up, the enemy often brings thoughts of fear, hopelessness and despair against your mind to make you want to stay in bed. What thoughts are plaguing, and even paralyzing, you from arising to take your position as the world-changer God needs you to be?

_____

_____

_____

_____

_____

> "Forget about what's happened; don't keep going over old history.
> Be alert, be present. I'm about to do something brand-new.
> It's bursting out! Don't you see it? There it is! I'm making
> a road through the desert, rivers in the badlands."
> **~Isaiah 43:18-19 The Message**

4. If you're living life tied to your past or under the enemy's control, it's time to break free! God offers you deliverance and a *new beginning* through Jesus. Write down any painful experiences you can't seem to break free from and surrender them to God in prayer.

_____

_____

_____

_____

_____

_____

Read and reflect on 1 Peter 5:7, Isaiah 43:18-19 and Philippians 3:13-15; then, jot down in the "Notes" section anything the Lord speaks to you about dealing with painful past experiences like these.

The Deliverance Process

"Emotional hurts and bondage usually come off in layers, just the way they got there in the first place. …Just as with giving birth to a baby, the worst pain comes right before the greatest deliverance of our lives. Things are the most difficult right before the biggest blessing is about to come forth. But God's timing is perfect. If women were able to deliver babies whenever we wanted to, we would deliver them sometime in the second month when the morning sickness kicked in. But the baby would not survive because it would be premature. The same is true with deliverance. We have to provide the best conditions we can, give it time, and try not to do anything to terminate it once the process has been set in motion."
~Stormie Omartian[3]

step three: ATTIRE

To dress yourself or somebody else, especially in clothes of a particular type.[4] In this instance, the clothes referred to are "clothes of light"—the light of God's Word.

5. Once you're awake and have risen to begin the day, the next step is to *get dressed*. But before you can put on *day* clothes, you must take off your *night* clothes. Read Romans 13:12. Are there any "dark deeds" that seem to continually cling to you that you need to take off? If so, what are they?

_____

_____

_____

_____

_____

6. Just like firemen put on protective clothes, shoes and head gear before entering a fire, you *must* put on special spiritual clothes to protect yourself from the fiery attacks of the enemy. Carefully read Ephesians 6:11-18. What do these verses speak to you? Do you need to make any adjustments in the way you have been dressing spiritually?

_____

_____

_____

_____

_____

~Ephesians 6:12 The Message

step four: AWARE

To be mindful that something exists because you notice it or realize that it is happening.[5] Being aware means becoming conscious that God is *presently alive and active* in the world around you.

7. Who is God to *you*? What evidence are you holding onto that He is active in your life and the world around you?

_____

_____

_____

_____

_____

_____

8. One of the greatest hindrances to truly *connecting* with your heavenly Father is *doubt*. What things cause you to doubt God's goodness, love and faithfulness? On the other hand, what causes you to trust Him more and actually *strengthens* your faith?

_____

_____

_____

_____

_____

_____

May you really come …to know [practically, through experience for yourselves]
the love of Christ, which far surpasses mere knowledge [without experience];
that you may be filled [through all your being] unto all the fullness of God
[may have the richest measure of the divine Presence, and become
a body wholly filled and flooded with God Himself]!
~Ephesians 3:19 AMP
[Words in italics added for clarity.]

step five: **ATTITUDE**

A physical posture, either conscious or unconscious, especially while interacting with others.[6] Attitude includes setting your mental and emotional posture to be absent of doubt.

> And be constantly renewed in the spirit of your mind
> **[having a fresh mental and spiritual attitude]**, and put on the
> new nature (the regenerate self) created in God's image,
> [Godlike] in true righteousness and holiness.
> **~Ephesians 4:23-24 AMP**
> [Bold added for emphasis.]

9.   Without question, your *attitude* can make or break you. Interestingly, no one can force an attitude on you—you and you alone have the *right* and *responsibility* to choose it. Describe your attitude—your mental and emotional posture— toward God. Is it negative and filled with doubt, or is it positive and filled with faith to believe for the impossible?

_____
_____
_____
_____
_____
_____
_____

10.   Having a song in your heart, especially in the midst of difficult times, can power- fully impact your attitude and outlook on life. David knew this and wrote many Psalms as a result. Is there a certain Psalm that is a source of encouragement to you in light of what you are going through? If so, which one is it and why?

_____
_____
_____
_____
_____
_____
_____

If you don't have a favorite Psalm, check out these.

If you need to...	Take time to carefully read...
Enter into God's presence	Psalm 29; 95; 96; 100
Learn and think about God's goodness	Psalm 1; 19; 24; 133; 136; 139
Praise and thank the Lord	Psalm 8; 97; 103; 107; 113; 145; 150
Repent and ask God to forgive you of sin	Psalm 32; 51; 103
Find help and hope in times of trouble	Psalm 3; 14; 22; 37; 42; 46; 53; 116
Increase your confidence and trust in God	Psalm 23; 40; 91; 121; 127
Get direction for decisions you must make	Psalm 25

Activity

Write your name in the blank of each personalized Scripture and then take a few minutes to meditate on these promises to *you* from God.

Behold! I have given you, _____, authority and power to trample upon serpents and scorpions, and [physical and mental strength and ability] over all the power that the enemy [possesses]; and nothing shall in any way harm you.

~**Luke 10:19 AMP**

...overwhelming victory is yours, _____, through Christ, who loved you. And I am convinced that nothing can ever separate you, _____, from God's love. Neither death nor life, neither angels nor demons, neither your fears for today nor your worries about tomorrow—not even the powers of hell can separate you from God's love. No power in the sky above or in the earth below—indeed, nothing in all creation will ever be able to separate you from the love of God that is revealed in Christ Jesus your Lord.

~**Romans 8:37-39 NLT vs.2**

But thanks be to God, Who in Christ always leads you, _____, in triumph [as trophies of Christ's victory].... For the weapons of your warfare, _____, are not physical [weapons of flesh and blood], but they are mighty before God for the overthrow and destruction of strongholds.

~**2 Corinthians 2:14, 10:4 AMP**

How we praise God, the Father of our Lord Jesus Christ, who has blessed you, _____, with every blessing in heaven because you belong to Christ.

~**Ephesians 1:3 TLB**

You, _____, are from God and have overcome them, because the one who is in you, _____, is greater than the one who is in the world. ...for everyone born of God, including you, _____, overcomes the world. This is the victory that has overcome the world, even your faith.

~1 John 4:4, 5:4 NIV

What are these Scriptures speaking to you? How do they affect your attitude toward God?

_____

_____

_____

_____

_____

Your PART

"You need to get the attitude that you bring solution to every problem you encounter. In the Word of God, there is solution... We need to be women that when we arrive, darkness flees and light comes. We need to out-rank everything in the spirit. When we come on the scene, we do not need to be afraid of anything because we have the attitude 'I am the daughter of the Most High God. Demons, you need to tremble and be afraid.'"

[adapted from session 6]

It is very important to keep a positive attitude full of faith and power. How can you maintain such a mindset? By hiding the promises of God's Word in your heart. It is the energy of God's living Word that nurtures and fuels the fire of our dreams. No other book on earth possesses the power to transform your life. Write key verses out in a notebook, on index cards, or type them on a computer. As you follow God's instruction in Joshua 1:8 and saturate your spirit and soul with truth, your life will be transformed!

step six: ASSET

Somebody or something that is useful and contributes to the success of something.[7] Seeing yourself as an asset means you realize you are a vital part of the victory and you know that you bring answers to life's problems everywhere you go.

11. How do you see yourself—as an *asset* or a *liability*? Do you view yourself as a blessing and an answer, or a trouble and trial to others? Explain.

_____

_____

_____

_____

12. If you don't see yourself as an asset, why? What has held you back from being a solution to something or someone?

_____

_____

_____

_____

step seven: **APPROACH**

To move closer to somebody or something.[8] God desires you to approach Him boldly—to move closer to Him by declaring His might and supremacy.

13. As you approach God in prayer, begin to *magnify* Him and minimize your problem. In other words, don't keep talking about and rehearsing how bad everything seems to be—tell God the problem and then talk about how good He is and thank Him for helping you. Write out a brief prayer of praise and thanks to the Lord for His awesomeness and goodness to you.

Planting **PRINCIPLE**

"You are an asset to this world. You, beautiful one, are an answer, not a problem. Actually, daughter, you are a part of the solution to the human crisis. There is a gift deep within only you can give. You must find this strength, this talent, this ability and give it to others."

[pages 230, 231]

_____

_____

_____

_____

_____

May all those who seek, inquire of and for You, and require You
[as their vital need] rejoice and be glad in You; and may those who love
Your salvation say continually, **Let God be magnified!**
~Psalm 70:4 AMP
[Bold added for emphasis.]

14.   Don't let Satan use *condemnation* and *guilt* over past sins to steal your joy and peace or keep you from approaching the courts of your Creator. Jesus paid the price for you to have *open access* to the Father's throne anytime, anywhere, about anything.

Escape the clutches of condemnation! Hide in your heart God's promises found in Romans 8:1 and John 3:17-18. What do these Scriptures speak to you *personally*?

_____

_____

_____

Exercise your open access to God's throne through Christ! Hide in your heart God's promises found in Hebrews 4:15-16 and Ephesians 3:12. What do these Scriptures speak to you *personally*?

_____

_____

_____

step eight: **ASK**

To put a question to somebody. To make a request for something.[9] To ask God for something means to boldly petition heaven for your needs and the needs of others.

15.   When you're in need of something—large or small, spiritual or natural—God is the *first* person you should run to for help. If He isn't, why? What is keeping you from going straight to Him for help? Pray and ask Him to reveal it to you.

_____

_____

_____

_____

_____

16. God yearns for you to fearlessly, confidently and consistently approach His throne and *ask* Him for things that you and others need—things that are confirmed in His Word. What have you been asking God for lately? Write down the most memorable prayer God answered and how it has affected your life and the lives of others.

_____

_____

_____

_____

_____

_____

If you live in Me [abide vitally united to Me] and My words remain in you and
continue to live in your hearts, ask whatever you will, and it shall be done for you.
When you bear (produce) much fruit, My Father is honored and glorified,
and you show and prove yourselves to be true followers of Mine.
~John 15:7-8 AMP

17. Read Matthew 7:7-8. What do you think happens if you **don't** *ask, seek* or *knock*? What should always be the motivating reason for asking God for anything? (Check out John 14:13-14.)

_____

_____

_____

_____

_____

_____

18. Write down some BIG prayers that you have been believing God for or have simply not asked for yet.

_____

_____

_____

_____

_____

_____

Your **PART**

"Daughter, sister, mother, friend, I fear we ask too little because we think too small. Perhaps we have felt isolated, inconsequential, weak, feminine, and inadequate, but nothing is farther from the truth. You are powerful and your questions are essential. ...We have the promise of the Holy Spirit to lead us. His words will rightly divide our motives and when we ask anything birthed in this dynamic, it will be granted or arranged. ...There is something this world needs that only you know how to ask for. You are the one to see the situation and entreat heaven. Beautiful daughters, ask!"

[adapted from pages 237, 238]

step nine: **ACT**

The action of carrying something out; in this case, to actually carry out God's plan on the earth.[10]

**You are writing one aspect of heaven's involvement
on earth each and every day.**

Activity

Star Search

"'Men and women who have lived wisely and well will shine brilliantly, like the cloudless, star-strewn night skies. And those who put others on the right path to life will glow like stars forever.'"
~Daniel 12:3 The Message

Before Jesus ascended into heaven, He commissioned all His followers—including you and me—to go and make disciples of all nations (see Matthew 28:19-20). To a great degree, this is simply impacting and influencing the lives of others for Christ both near and far.

Look around you. What women do you know who look up to you with admiration and respect? Who asks you for advice from time to time and actually puts it into practice? These are the daughters of heaven who are *open* vessels who God wants you to pour into. Daughter of the Most High, time is short—the Lord's return is near. Don't waste your resources and energy trying to pour into people who are closed to you—help those who want to be helped.

Make it your aim to actively look for one woman each month in whom you can invest. She may be in the church choir, women's ministry or youth ministry. She may be a neighbor down the block. Never fear; God will make it clear whom He wants you to minister to. Take her to lunch or invite her over to your house for a time of fellowship. As she speaks, *listen* to her heart. Encourage her, share Scriptures with her that have helped you, pray for her, and if possible, anoint her to be used of God to begin nurturing other women in her sphere of influence.

Run Well

Jesus, undeterred, went right ahead and gave his charge: "God authorized and commanded me to commission you: Go out and train everyone you meet, far and near, in this way of life…."

~Matthew 28:19 The Message

Daughter of the Most High, the time has come for you to take action. This is your moment in history to make a decision to walk away from all that holds you back and step into your future. You have a divine destiny to fulfill—to help unleash the gift of nurture in the captive women

Planting PRINCIPLE

"The world is not happening to us—we are happening to it. The light is far more powerful than the darkness and it is time we acted as if this was true. We need to lose the Christian escape-the-world mentality and be those who overcome in this world."

[page 230]

of the earth. In Christ you are much bigger and more powerful than you know…your prayers and actions are more potent to change the world than you can imagine. There are problems only *you* can help solve—questions that only *you* can help answer.

A new day is dawning in your life. **It's time** to *awake* and *arise* to the promised opportunities set before you. **It's time** to *attire* yourself in God's armor and become *aware* of His activity all around you. **It's time** to adjust your *attitude*, letting the overcoming mind of Christ rule and reign within you. Realize you are an indispensable *asset* to God's plan for victory. *Approach* His throne boldly and *ask* for what you and others need. **It's time** to step out of your comfort zone and take *action*!

"I command you—be strong and courageous! Do not be afraid or discouraged.
For the Lord your God is with you wherever you go."

~Joshua 1:9

**Run well daughter.
You are watched for, loved and well-able.**

Here you are at the end of this study on nurture. To experience lasting change, truth must be applied to your life and coupled with consistent, Spirit-led *action*. What action(s) is the Holy Spirit prompting you to take?

Prayer

Thank You, Father, for this eye-opening message on nurture. I commit myself to You afresh today. Use me, Lord, to create connections with those around me, starting with my own family. Open my eyes to those who are open to You. Help me to not be so busy that I miss the opportunities You bring to me to pour into someone else's life and impact them for eternity. Show me how to be an answer to the problems of others—empower me to bring solutions wherever I go. May everything I've learned become deeply rooted in my spirit and soul and be used to bring forth lasting fruit in my life and the lives of others. In Jesus' name, Amen!

Take some time to hear what the Lord is speaking to you. Write down what He is revealing.

_____

_____

_____

_____

_____

_____

_____

_____

_____

_____

1. Adapted from definitions appearing in *Nurture*, Lisa Bevere (Faith Words, New York, NY 2008) pp.223-239. 2. See note 1, p.227. 3. Stormie Omartian, *The Power of a Praying Husband* (Harvest House Publishers, Eugene, OR 2001) pp. 196,197. 4. See note 1, p.228. 5. See note 1, p.228. 6. See note 1, p.229. 7. See note 1, p.230. 8. See note 1, p.231. 9. See note 1, p.232. 10. See note 1, p.239.

notes from session 6

notes

notes

For **more** information
        please contact us:

Messenger
International®

life-transforming truth.

SIGN UP
to receive e-mails from John & Lisa Bevere
Visit us online at
www.MessengerInternational.org

united states
PO BOX 888
PALMER LAKE, CO 80133-0888

800.648.1477 *us and canada
T: 719.487.3000

mail@MessengerInternational.org

europe
PO BOX 1066
HEMEL HEMPSTEAD
HP2 7GQ
UNITED KINGDOM

T: 0800 9808 933
(OUTSIDE UK)
T: +44 1442 288 531

uk@MessengerInternational.org

australia
ROUSE HILL TOWN CENTRE
P.O. BOX 6444
ROUSE HILL NSW 2155

T: 1.300.650.577
(OUTSIDE AUS)
T: +61 2 9679 4900

aus@MessengerInternational.org

Books by Lisa

Be Angry, But Don't Blow It!
Fight Like a Girl
Kissed the Girls and Made Them Cry
Nurture
Out of Control and Loving It!
The True Measure of a Woman
You Are Not What You Weigh

nur✝ure

Give and Get What You Need to Flourish

Nurture is what you need to give and get! As God's daughters, it is our season to flourish! This curriculum positions you to make connections, write your life, reclaim your feminine intuition, strengthen your family and find your place as the world-changer God has destined you to be. Nurture is not merely taught, but modeled throughout these seven DVD sessions. You and your group will be encouraged by Darlene Zschech, Joyce Meyer, Jack Hayford, Bobbie Houston, and 13 other leaders from around the globe who have lent their strength to this project. You will be inspired, encouraged and empowered through this life-transforming curriculum experience.

Curriculum Includes:

- 7 Sessions on 3 DVDs & 3 CDs (30 minutes each)
- Hardcover Book
- Devotional Workbook
- Encouraging Videos from 17 international leaders
- Promotional Materials
- Cross Necklace: Adjustable 16-18 inch Genuine Swarovski Crystal Necklace

Beautiful Daughter, this world needs you, so find your voice and bring your strength!

Fight Like *a Girl*
The Power of Being a Woman

You are an answer, not a problem.

Curriculum Includes:

- 12 Video Lessons on 4 DVDs (30 minutes each)
- Hardcover Book
- Devotional Workbook
- Promotional Materials & Bookmark
- Makeup Bag
- Bracelet – Genuine Swarovski Austrian Crystal

In *Fight Like a Girl*, Lisa challenges the status quo that women need to fit into the role of a man, and she leads you in the truth of what it means to be a woman. Discover how to express your God-given strengths and fulfill your role in the community, workplace, home and church. This curriculum will encourage you to find your true potential and realize you are an answer and not a problem.

KISSED THE GIRLS AND MADE THEM CRY

Curriculum Includes:

- 4 Video Lessons & Bonus Q&A on 2 DVDs (50-60 minutes each)
- Best-selling Book
- Devotional Workbook
- Promotional Materials

Don't believe the lie—sexual purity isn't about rules...it's about freedom and power. It is time to take back what we've cheaply given away. This kit is for women of all ages who long for a greater intimacy with Jesus and need to embrace God's healing and restoring love.

"I'm 15, and through your kit my nightmare has been turned back to a dream!"

Beautiful - DVD

Part of being beautiful and authentic is realizing the value of you, the original! An original is the beginning of something. You were never meant to be defined by others and reduced to a pseudo copy or forgery. Do you know there is something extremely unique and beautiful only you have? Whether you embrace your uniqueness or live out your life as only a mixed blend of the lives of others is really up to you. But know this – the whole world is watching in the hope that you will be a beautiful original.

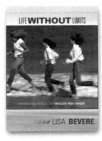

Life Without Limits - DVD

It is definitely no longer about us, but about Him! God is calling a generation of women who are willing to take risks and go out over their heads in Him. Women brave enough to trust Him with every area of their life. He is watching for wild women who will be reckless in both their abandonment to God and their commitment to obedience. It is time to embrace His freedom in every area. This powerful and dynamic video was recorded at a women's mentoring conference and will empower you in these crucial areas:
- Completing versus competing
- Making your marriage a place of power
- Refining and defining your motivation
- Harnessing your power of influence
- Answering the mandate

The Power of Two with One Heart - CD

God never intended our marriages to be something we endure, but a beautiful and exciting haven where both the man and woman flourish.

In *The Power of Two with One Heart*, Lisa calls out to both men and women to see God's original plan for marriage and to take back what has been lost. When we embrace our roles and lend our strengths, it is then the restoration can begin.

With God, it's always been about one man, one woman, one heart.

Extreme Makeover - 2 CD SET

Makeovers of every kind are the current craze. Not only are faces and bodies being hauled over, but everything is subject to this before-and-after experimentation. People just can't seem to get enough, and rather than judging, the church needs to ask the all-important question...Why? I believe it is because we are all desperate for change!

It's Time - CD

For too long we have had the attitude, "It's my turn!" But when God begins to pour out His spirit, it is nobody's turn; it becomes everybody's time. It is time for God's gifts in His body to come forth. The Father is gifting men and women alike to shine in each and every realm of life. Discover what He has placed in your hand and join the dance of a lifetime.